PENGUIN BOOKS

Strictly Bipolar

'A timely book. Darian Leader's thoughts are more interesting, more humane and more persuasive than the profit-fixated strong-arm coercion of the madness industry. Instead of the shoddy reasoning that leads to wrong treatment and over-treatment, he offers illumination and insight; his book is a contribution to a debate, but it could also change lives' Hilary Mantel

D1340240

ABOUT THE AUTHOR

Darian Leader is a psychoanalyst practising in London and a member of the Centre for Freudian Analysis and Research and of the College of Psychoanalysts – UK. His books include *Why Do Women Write More Letters Than They Post?*, *Freud's Footnotes*, *Stealing the Mona Lisa*, *The New Black: Mourning, Melancholia and Depression*, *What is Madness?* and, with David Corfield, *Why Do People Get Ill?* He is Honorary Visiting Professor in the School of Human and Life Sciences, Roehampton University.

Strictly Bipolar

DARIAN LEADER

PENGUIN BOOKS

PENGUIN BOOKS

Published by the Penguin Group
Penguin Books Ltd, 80 Strand, London WC2R ORL, England
Penguin Group (USA) Inc., 375 Hudson Street, New York, New York 10014, USA
Penguin Group (Canada), 90 Eglinton Avenue East, Suite 700, Toronto, Ontario, Canada M4P 2Y3
(a division of Pearson Penguin Canada Inc.)
Penguin Ireland, 25 St Stephen's Green, Dublin 2, Ireland (a division of Penguin Books Ltd)
Penguin Group (Australia), 707 Collins Street, Melbourne, Victoria 3008, Australia
(a division of Pearson Australia Group Pty Ltd)
Penguin Books India Pvt Ltd, 11 Community Centre, Panchsheel Park, New Delhi – 110 017, India
Penguin Group (NZ), 67 Apollo Drive, Rosedale, Auckland 0632, New Zealand
(a division of Pearson New Zealand Ltd)
Penguin Books (South Africa) (Pty) Ltd, Block D, Rosebank Office Park,
181 Jan Smuts Avenue, Parktown North, Gauteng 2193, South Africa

Penguin Books Ltd, Registered Offices: 80 Strand, London WC2R ORL, England

www.penguin.com

First published 2013
001

Set in 11/13pt Dante MT Std
Typeset by Jouve (UK), Milton Keynes
Printed in Great Britain by Clays Ltd, St Ives plc

ISBN: 978-0-241-14610-1

www.greenpenguin.co.uk

ALWAYS LEARNING   **PEARSON**

For L, S and Y

Contents

If the post-war period was called the 'age of anxiety' and the 80s and 90s the 'antidepressant era', we now live in bipolar times. A diagnosis that once applied to less than 1% of the population has risen dramatically, with almost 25% of Americans estimated to suffer from some form of bipolarity. Mood-stabilizing medication is routinely prescribed to adults and children alike, with child prescriptions increasing by 400% and the overall diagnosis by 4,000% since the mid-90s. The question today is not 'Are you bipolar?' but 'How bipolar are you?'

Celebrities like Catherine Zeta-Jones, Stephen Fry, Jean-Claude Van Damme, Demi Lovato, Adam Ant, Tom Fletcher and Linda Hamilton speak of their bipolar conditions, and both memoirs and self-help books flood the marketplace. CIA agent Carrie Mathison in *Homeland* and ex-teacher Pat Solitano in *Silver Linings Playbook* are portrayed as bipolar, and it even receives a mention in the children's cartoon *Scooby-Doo*.

Business manuals meanwhile advocate the cultivation of a certain degree of mania in order to play the markets, and executives are actually taught how to ride a manic high to increase sales and productivity. A media image depicts mogul Ted Turner as a furiously determined sea captain, with the warning that he has come off lithium, so his competitors should beware! In Hollywood, stars visit their psychiatrists with agent in tow, the latter making sure that the medication works to keep the mania down but not *too* down: more than anywhere else, we witness here the tailoring of a drugs regime to suit the requirements of career and lifestyle.

The confidence, exhilaration and energy that characterize the early phases of mania seem so well suited to the exhortations to achievement, productivity and intense commitment that today's businesses demand. In a fiercely competitive world where job stability and security are increasingly eroded, employees have to prove their worth by working longer and longer hours and professing ever-more ecstatic belief in their projects and products. The inevitable days off due to exhaustion and depletion are seen less as evidence that something is wrong than as almost a part of one's job description.

At the same time, the very features that classical psychiatry ascribed to the manic attack emerge as the aims of personal development. Self-help books and therapies promote the ideas of self-esteem, heightened self-confidence and well-being. Nothing is impossible, they tell us, we must follow our dreams. And if the cardinal symptom of mania was once defined as the compulsive quest to connect with other human beings, today this is almost an obligation: if you're not on Facebook or Twitter, there must be something wrong with you. What were once the clinical signs of manic-depressive psychosis have now become the goals of therapies and lifestyle coaching.

Yet beyond the new incitements to 'manic' behaviour, those with manic-depression describe the terrible lows and nightmarish states of agitation that accompany their episodes. The feelings of power, confidence and connect-edness that characterize mania make the person feel supremely alive while at the same time bringing them closer than ever before to death. The paradox of bi-polarity has been observed time and time again: ask a manic-depressive subject if they could push a button and make their bipolarity disappear and many will say No. Yet these same people may regularly end up in hospital, having squandered their savings in a massive shopping spree, wounded their family through abandon or neg-lect, or risked their life in some ill-starred act of heroism or hedonism.

How can we make sense of the new ubiquity of bipolar selves? Are the highs and lows of bipolarity a consequence of changing economic conditions, with sustained bursts of energy replacing the more traditional image of the stable exercise of a profession? And beyond the often shallow talk of workplace 'mania', is there a real bipolarity beyond this, the same one that psychia-trists used to call manic-depression? Bipolarity might seem to fit the strange and convulsive rhythms of early-twenty-first-century life, yet, as anyone who has the experience of manic-depression will tell you, it is a serious thing.

—

A hundred years ago, the term 'bipolar' was exceedingly rare. It was first used in psychiatry in the late nineteenth century, yet gained its prominence from the 80s onwards until it became a household word in the 90s. How did this newfound popularity come about? Historians of psychiatry have all made the same observation here. It was precisely when the patents began to run out on the biggest-selling mainstream antidepressants in the mid-90s that bipolar suddenly became the recipient of the vast marketing budgets of the pharmaceutical industry.

Websites helped people to diagnose themselves, journal articles and supplements appeared all referring to bipolar as if it were a fact: and nearly all of these were funded, in whole or in part, by the pharmaceutical industry. Internet questionnaires allowed self-diagnosis in a few minutes, and, for many people, it seemed as if their difficulties finally had a name. Just as in the 80s so many people at last understood that they were afflicted with 'depression', now 'bipolar' became the label to designate the suffering felt by a new generation.

The irony here was that in those cases where the antidepressant drugs clearly didn't work, it was now claimed that their failure was due to the fact that they had been wrongly prescribed. The patients were actually bipolar, yet the subtle mood changes had been missed by the prescribing physician. Between 20% and 35% of those diagnosed with depression in primary care have now been deemed to suffer from bipolar disorder. As the psychiatrist David Healy points out, rather than trying to make more effective antidepressants, the industry opted to market a new brand: a new set of disorders called 'bipolar' rather than a new medication.

This colonization required a burgeoning of bipolar categories. Bipolar 1 was often equated with classical manic-depression, but Bipolar 2 lowered the threshold dramatically, requiring merely one depressive episode and one period of increased productivity, inflated self-esteem and reduced need for sleep. Bipolar 2.5, 3, 3.5, 4, 5 and 6 soon followed. An increasing emphasis on mood fluctuations rather than on underlying processes meant that more and more people could be caught on the bipolar compass. Today, there is even 'soft bipolar', which means that the patient 'responds strongly to losses'. This loosening of diagnostic boundaries generated a colossal expansion of the pharmaceutical market and extended an open invitation to consumers to see themselves as bipolar.

A category – Bipolar 3 – was even invented to designate those whose bipolarity had been revealed by antidepressants. Taking antidepressant drugs such as Prozac intensified the manic states, thus showing the true diagnosis and indicating that a new mood-stabilizing medication should be taken. It is a fact that thousands of people experienced states of agonizing agitation and racing, intrusive thoughts after starting some of the anti-depressant drugs, yet there is clearly a big difference between seeing these states as isolated effects of the drug or as a core condition which the drugs simply unveiled.

The rabbit in the hat was that the anticonvulsant sodium valproate (Depakote) received a patent for use in treating mania at exactly the time that the earlier anti-depressant patents were expiring. Just as depression had been actively marketed as a disorder by those who pur-veyed a chemical cure for it, so bipolar was packaged and sold along with its remedy. Lithium had worked for some and not for others, yet, as a naturally occurring element, it could not be patented. Valproate was initially pro-claimed the smarter and more reliable drug, the one that would finally stabilize the highs and lows of the bipolar subject. It was swiftly joined by new-generation anti-psychotic drugs such as olanzapine, now licensed for use in bipolar.

Many people have found valproate helpful, just as many people feel that they owe their life to the right dose of lithium, but the problem here is that the new cartography of mental health came at a price. The more the diagnoses of bipolarity increased, the more the old category of manic-depression became lost or, at best, confused. A once-specific diagnosis was transformed into an ever-more vague spectrum of disorders, and there was one crucial mistake here, which early, pre-twentieth-century psychiatry had pinpointed in the very minting of the terms that would later become equated with the label 'bipolar'.

In the 1840s, the French psychiatrists Jean-Pierre Falret and Jules Baillarger had introduced the terms 'circular madness' and 'double form madness'. The standard histories usually have it that these concepts then became the 'manic-depressive insanity' conceptualized by Emil Kraepelin and then appropriated by Western psychiatry as 'bipolar disorder'. Yet in fact the key arguments made by Falret and Baillarger were quite the opposite of Kraepelin's and, indeed, of the later psychiatrists. Their diagnostic categories were intended to show that highs and lows were not in themselves constitutive of the new entity they were trying to describe. Their careful work aimed to separate a specific type of 'madness' from what appeared to be mania and depression in other disorders.

This reflects quite accurately what we encounter

clinically. Anyone can become loud, agitated, restless, hyperactive and even dangerous, given the right – or the wrong – conditions. If a paranoiac person, for example, feels he has an important message to deliver to mankind and is then blocked in his attempts to broadcast it, he might become desperate. Inhibiting or arresting the effort to convey some truth of global or domestic gravity can produce a turmoil that is often confused with mania. Think, indeed, of the effects of being continually kept on hold at some telephone call centre and then being systematically misunderstood by its staff. The mixture of rage and apparent incoherence that this produces is precisely one of the classical senses of the term 'mania'.

Similarly, a schizophrenic person can become exquisitely elated and then experience a terrible state of dejection and despair. They may become boisterous and talkative, moving from one topic to another with apparent abandon. Sleep and food might be progressively neglected, and they may have the idea that they can influence others with their thoughts, for example. Such phenomena can now routinely be found in descriptions of bipolar, with the distinctions and differentiations made by the early psychiatrists neglected or simply forgotten.

Falret and Baillarger's predecessor Jean-Étienne Esquirol had done his best to deprive the term 'mania' of what he saw as its loose and casual meaning, and as the nineteenth century progressed it was distinguished from states of elation, excitement and agitated mental confusion. It has been observed, in fact, that the progressive abandonment of the use of physical restraints in asylums coincides with a decrease in the use of this word.

The less the patient was actually stopped from moving, the less he would be described as 'manic', suggesting that the term so often had a reactive sense: one became manic precisely because one was being obstructed or restrained in some way.

The same applied to depression. As Falret and Baillarger knew, anyone could become despondent and low in spirits. Wasn't this in fact one of the very consequences of having one's 'manic' activity kept in check for long enough? But the lows of the new clinical entity they were describing were different. There would be less insistence on a single theme or complaint, less the fixity on one unique object, such as a lost loved one, found in melancholia. The latter term refers not to the mood of self-absorbed sadness but to a specific form of psychosis in which the person remains caught in an unrelenting onslaught of self-reproach and castigation, which they will often broadcast to those around them.

What the Continental psychiatrists showed was how high and low moods were not in themselves constitutive of the manic-depressive structure they were trying to circumscribe. It was less a question of elation and misery than of the quality of such states, the relation between them and, most importantly, the thought processes underlying them. There was an effort to move beyond the vagaries of mood fluctuation and surface behaviour to find the latent motifs of manic-depression, and to investigate the difference that these might have to melancholia and other diagnostic categories.

Sadly, these classificatory efforts were undermined by Kraepelin, who argued that mania and melancholia, whether seen together or individually, were all part of the same 'disease'. The highs and lows that had been so carefully disentangled by the French psychiatrists were now lumped together in the overinclusive new category that Kraepelin initially promoted, and which is still largely promulgated by the standard texts of mainstream Western psychiatry as 'bipolar disorder'. Yet if we hope to differentiate true manic-depression from the many forms of bipolar that swamp the diagnostic marketplace, we need to go back to the original project of distinguishing its elations and depressions from those found in other kinds of mental structure.

———

Acknowledging the problems with the diagnosis of bipolar illuminates also the embarrassment of multiplying diagnoses and medications for the same person. A patient explained to me recently that they took lithium for their mania, olanzapine for their psychosis, dexmethylphenidate for their attention, and sertraline for their lows, as if their very being had been divided up on the table of an anatomist. Old psychiatry would have ridiculed such a dissection, recognizing that there is such a thing as manic-depressive psychosis, which includes within it mania and often depressions, and that one cannot divide up the person in such a way and prescribe for each symptom as if they were all unconnected.

Yet today this atomization, with its piecemeal regime of prescriptions, is the rule rather than the exception. In his memoir, *Electroboy*, the New York art dealer Andy Behrman details the thirty-two pills and capsules he was taking each day, at age thirty-four: Risperdal, an anti-psychotic; Depakote, a mood stabilizer; Neurontin, an anticonvulsant; Klonopin for anxiety; BuSpar, also for anxiety; Ambien to aid sleep; and then three further medications to counter the side effects of the others: Symmetrel for Parkinsonian syndrome; Propanolol for tremors; and Benadryl for muscle stiffness. All of this was the result of years of 'trial and error', as if what mattered were the parts of the person rather than the whole.

Both body and psyche are seen today as aggregates, with psychiatric intervention aiming to target isolated symptoms, and lifestyle coaching to add or subtract desired or unwanted aspects of the self. The American writer Lizzie Simon, who received a bipolar diagnosis in her teens, would later travel the country talking to others who had shared similar experiences. When one of her interviewees tells her, 'I'm strictly bipolar. I have nothing else going on,' it is in this context of a medical and cultural framework which ceaselessly divides up, which always searches for more symptoms to be segregated and then excised, without recognizing the link between them.

What this means is that medical staff are almost wholly concerned with fine-tuning medication, finding just the right balance of drugs that will work for the patient and achieve the best emotional balance. The effects of drugs, their side effects and compatibilities may be discussed in minute detail. Patients may feel involved and cared for in these interactions, but there is an elephant in the room: the whole conversation is about what the drugs are making them feel rather than what their original feelings had been before taking the drugs.

Once one enters the pharmaceutical marketplace, there is often little hope of return, as treatment priorities are focused around the search for the cocktail that will work best. Yet those diagnosed with bipolar have the highest rate of non-compliance of any patient group, a fact that generates endless rhetoric from both medical and patient-support groups on the importance of taking the pills. Why the non-compliance? Is it due to the unpleasant side effects of the drugs?

It's true that lithium and other drugs are hardly silver bullets: the person may feel disconnected from their self, sluggish or strangely absent. There may be weight gain and all manner of other problems that further drugs will then aim to regulate. On the other hand, there are some people who experience few such side effects and who make no protest about their regimes. Yet the reporting of side effects, or indeed the non-effects, of some drugs is notoriously unreliable. We know that poorer people are less likely to complain of side effects than wealthier ones, and that doctors only report adverse effects here to regulators in one case per 100. As David Healy observes, this makes the tracking of a parcel we send in the post more accurate today than the monitoring of the effects of a drug that we might be taking every day of our lives.

There is also the possibility that non-compliance is due to both the attraction of being in the early stages of mania and a denial of its ravaging effects. A manic episode can give someone a sense of being genuinely alive and connected to the world, of having found one's true identity for the first time. This may be difficult to give up, and in the intervals between manias, or between manias and depressions, there may also be an amnesia of the agony of manic burn-up or the splintering pain of the depressive low.

These are questions that it would be unwise to ignore, as they force us to think about the person's relation to the phenomena of manic-depression, rather than simply about how good or bad the drugs are. Instead of asking if some medication tempers racing thoughts or desperate agitation, we must ask what those thoughts actually were and how they came to overwhelm that person. If someone spends thousands of pounds in a shopping spree, we must ask what they bought and why. If they claim to have a fail-safe plan for a new global business, we must ask what this is and how the idea came to them. Such time-consuming and detailed work is the only way we will learn more about manic-depression. Where drugs aim to control and manage behaviour, an analytic approach aims to understand it and, hopefully, use this understanding to find new ways to help the person on the knife-edge of experiences that can be both so terrifying and so exhilarating, so life-affirming and yet also so lethal.

———

Let's start with mania. If we disassociate the term from those states of restlessness, desperation and turbulence that it had so often been used to describe in the past, what do we find instead? For Andy Behrman, who has richly documented the spirals of manic-depression, his mind 'teems with rapidly changing ideas and needs; my head is cluttered with vibrant colours, wild images, bizarre thoughts, sharp details, secret codes, symbols, and foreign languages. I want to devour everything – parties, people, magazines, books, music, art, movies and television.'

Being in a manic episode for Behrman 'is like having the most perfect prescription eyeglasses with which to see the world. Everything is precisely outlined . . . my senses are so heightened, I'm so awake and alert that my eyelashes fluttering on the pillow sound like thunder.' For Terri Cheney, the manic-depressive Beverly Hills attorney who gave up her highly paid work for mental health advocacy, mania 'lights up every nerve ending. The lightest sensation feels like a volcanic eruption.' The person wonders whether they had ever heard, touched or seen before, so different is their new perception of the world. It feels as if they had been born again, as if this were the very first day of their life.

For Stephen Fry, who writes of 'the freedom, expansiveness, energy and optimism' of mania, 'We are kings of the world, nothing is beyond us, society is too slow for our racing minds, everything is connected in a web of glorious colour, creativity and meaning.' A new confidence carries the manic subject. 'You can actually run faster,' says one manic-depressive man. 'What kind of illness does that? It shows what's within us, what we are capable of. We're all so deadened in our senses. Whatever else a manic person is, they are *alive*.' And this absolute vitality turbocharges speech. Talking becomes easy, words flow with a newfound fluency, there is no more silence. As Terri Cheney puts it, 'I wanted to talk, I needed to talk, words pressed up so hard against the roof of my mouth I felt like I had to spit to breathe.'

Ideas and projects abound, nothing seems impossible, and the manic person may embark on any number of creative or entrepreneurial schemes, spending large sums of money, which more often than not are borrowed from family, friends or banks. The future seems to hold so much promise, so many certainties of success, wealth and achievement. The excitement here is volitional, imbued with a burning sense of purpose.

The usual barriers that hold people back from risk-taking have vanished. No opponent or obstacle seems unbeatable or insurmountable. Things are going so well, a new lifestyle can in some cases crystallize almost overnight, often to the consternation and puzzlement of family and friends. From a modest bedsit the manic subject might move to a lavish West End apartment, dressing and dining like a millionaire. Bills are paid in cash, huge tips left in cafés and restaurants, conversations struck up almost anywhere, as if everyone were a potential best friend or lover.

Sexual encounters and propositions may multiply, yet usually with little wish for longevity. As these radical changes to pre-manic life burgeon, other people can become too present: frictions with sexual partners, or business associates or banks who want their money back, friends who get fed up with what appears to be narcissistic and self-indulgent behaviour, interlocutors who tire of acting as sounding boards for grand schemes and projects. The manic high becomes tinged with anxiety. Small impediments become magnified, triggering rages and violent outbursts. Paranoid thoughts increase. And now things have gone too far.

As one of Lizzie Simon's interviewees explained, 'I felt I was on a freight train. I couldn't steer it. I couldn't stop it.' In a terrifying image, the Scottish writer Brian Adams encapsulates this curve of mania in his savage memoir, *The Pits and the Pendulum*. After an evening carousing and singing at his local pub, he returns home and makes tea, feeling fine, still singing, when 'Suddenly I am clapping my hands together in wide swings, smashing the palms together as hard as I can: slowly, hard and uncontrollably.' Soon he is cutting up his arms and face with a Stanley knife. The temporary high has escalated into something unspeakably horrific. As one of my patients put it, mania is like a rocket, roaring splendidly and unstoppably into space, then disintegrating in bursts of fire, smoke and debris, like the ill-fated space shuttle he had watched on TV as a child.

To explore the experience of mania, we need to listen to these accounts carefully, avoiding vague equations of noisy or elated behaviour with mania as such. Several motifs seem ubiquitous here: the sense of connectedness with other people and with the world; the spending of money, which the person usually does not have; the large appetite, be it for food, sex or words; the reinvention of oneself, the creation of a new persona as if one were someone else; the verbal dexterity and sudden penchant for wit and punning; the movement towards paranoid thoughts, so apparently absent at the beginning of the manic curve.

Perhaps the most striking of these is the idea of a connection between things. The colours, images, symbols and codes evoked by Behrman matter less for what they are than for the fact of being linked together. In a mania, everything seems somehow purposefully connected, as if a vast join-the-dots puzzle has been suddenly completed, to reveal a figure that no one had noticed until then. As the American mental health advocate Calvin Dunn describes it in his autobiography, *Losing My Mind*, 'it seemed like everything meant something, every sound I heard and everything I saw, and it seemed like everything made sense and was connected in some way'.

Gazing at a brook in the gardens of UCLA, the research psychiatrist and writer Kay Redfield Jamison was reminded of a scene from Tennyson's poetry. Overtaken by 'an immediate and inflaming sense of urgency', she rushed off to a bookshop to find a copy, and soon had more than twenty books under her arms. The initial image of the Lady of the Lake had spiralled off, connecting to other themes and titles, from Malory's *Le Morte d'Arthur* to Frazer's *The Golden Bough* and books by Jung and Robert Graves. Everything seemed related, and together would contain 'some essential key' to the universe as she 'wove and wove' her manic web of associations.

The manic person feels a part of this, wonderfully linked to the world rather than being its slave or its servant. The exhilaration that the sense of connectedness brings must be *communicated*, a detail that serves to distinguish true mania from states of elation in other cases. A schizophrenic subject may quietly enjoy a state of beatitude alone in their room, but the manic-depressive will not only experience it but feel the necessity to share it with the world. Likewise, anyone can enter a state of exuberance or even hyperactivity, especially after an experience of loss, but although this may be diagnosed as mania or its milder cousin hypomania, the key is whether the person has a sense that things are connected or not. Do they just love the sound of the bird singing or, as well as loving it, do they feel it is linked to the car that went by or the article they read in the paper that morning?

How could one explain the powerful feeling of connectedness between things described so precisely and consistently by manic subjects? What, after all, is the medium of connectivity in our world? The answer to this question is perhaps disappointing in its simplicity: it is language. It is words, ideas and the associations between them that create and shape our realities, and we rely on both the links and the inhibition of links between them to be able to think. This becomes clearest when the links between ideas come at such a pace that one cannot even slow them down or stop them. In what psychiatry terms 'flight of ideas', one thought leads to another with an irrepressible, brutal persistence.

Think of the Internet game that allows one to see how any actor is linked in some way to the *Footloose* star Kevin Bacon. Every movie-industry figure will turn out to have a connection, either through an immediate association, such as working on one of Bacon's films, or through dealings with someone who came into contact with Bacon. The spectacular success of this game has led to it becoming a built-in feature of Google, and there is even a board game devoted to this curious pursuit. Mobile phone adverts, in turn, show how the whole universe can be connected to Bacon through verbal associations. But imagine if this associative quest was less a diversion or entertainment than a constant feature of one's existence that one could not turn off. As the Google feature and mobile adverts show, the sociolinguistic web of language and culture will always provide connections. There is no letting up.

Life, we could say, relies on us not asking how we are connected to Kevin Bacon too often. If we were compelled to follow every association, we would be overwhelmed by the vast web of connections that inevitably exists around us. But in mania, the network takes over. Nineteenth-century psychiatrists observed how the speech of the manic subject seemed to move from one word to another with little regard to content, as if the bridges between ideas came from language itself rather than from conscious deliberation. 'What a pretty tie,' says a patient, 'I wish I were tied to someone who was pure, and had pretty eyes. I'm fond of pretty eyes. Fond of lies.' The speech moves from the necktie, to the 'tie' as attachment, to the 'eye', and then the 'lie'. 'Bearing children is all very well when you have no bearing-down pains. There are too many panes in the window.' Although windows and childbirth might seem to have little in common, the 'pain' of delivery moves immediately to the 'pane' of window glass.

In contrast to these examples of manic speech, when depressed, the person would have little to say, and repeat words with the same basic signification: they were worthless, spiritually void, guilty of some terrible and ineradicable sin. There thus seemed to be a contrast between the way that in manic states the person was at the mercy of acoustic and formal connections between words but in the depressive states it was meaning or signification that governed them. Early researchers observed how in the depressed state the resonance between words – the movement from 'eye' to 'lie' and 'pain' to 'pane' – was hardly ever apparent, as if language had lost its acoustic vibrancy.

How strange that the two axes of language – words and meanings – would each emerge in manic-depression in alternating strengths, as if each would have to wait its turn before seizing their subject. In the mania, it seemed as if words had prised themselves away from their meanings, so that acoustic connections could be followed, whereas in the depressions words were few and loaded with a single, monolithic meaning. 'I'm a cunt', 'I'm a cunt', 'I'm a cunt', as one of my patients repeated to himself endlessly in the low phases of his manic-depression.

Clinically things are a bit more complicated than this contrast might suggest. Manic subjects don't just follow words freely since they tend to end up at the same ideas or words or significations, as if led back to the same points on a map. The range of ideas may in fact be quite limited, and it was even suggested to speak not of 'flight of ideas' but of 'flight of words', since it was speech that seemed to go on interminably, circumscribing a relatively small set of concerns. Early researchers such as Falret, Hugo Liepmann and Ludwig Binswanger showed that this flight of words followed a hidden logic that was lost upon the casual observer. Mania was never a purely random flow of words, but had a real coherence and structure, yet one that was usually not obvious unless one listened very carefully.

To take one example, when Norma Farnes visited the manic-depressive comedian Spike Milligan for the first time to apply for a job as his personal assistant, she remarked that the room was freezing. 'Yes,' he replied, 'I hate the Americans.' This apparently meaningless response could be taken as the sign of manic dispersal, an inability to engage in dialogue or to follow a thought through. Yet in fact, as Farnes would learn, it was absolutely coherent. She had commented on the room's temperature and Milligan believed that the Americans had invented central heating. The implicit chain was thus: it's freezing – the central heating isn't adequate – Americans invented central heating – I hate the Americans. Farnes, perhaps prudently, didn't question his syllogism by telling him that it was the Romans and not the Americans who were ultimately responsible for the invention of heating.

If manic speech is not as random as it may seem, what characterizes its apparent drift? Let's think about where manic states start. It is sometimes claimed that mania just triggers with no warning, as if completely out of the blue, yet often the manic person or those around him or her do sense in advance that something is changing, heralded perhaps by lack of sleep or anxiety. When the flight of ideas gets going, so often we find that it begins when the person is in a situation of dialogue, with colleagues, in a meeting, at a conference, in a bar with friends. Often there is a tinge of aggression or antagonsim, as if one member of the group is hostile to the person. But then an amazing thing happens.

Most people feel in social situations that they don't say the right thing, that words somehow fail them. Later, they can imagine what they could or ought to have said, in the famous *esprit d'escalier*: it is only afterwards as they are on the stairs that they realize. But a manic subject has a different experience. They have the words to say it. The actress Patty Duke refers to her 'incredible command of the language' when manic. As the academic Lisa Hermsen says of her own experience of mania, 'I found the words and typed the letters' – a feeling echoed time and time again by manic subjects. As one of my patients put it, 'The right words were just there, I didn't have to think any more.' And Cheney: 'The right words were just dancing in the air above my head, and I simply had to snatch them down and let them flow through my pen.'

Suddenly the manic person is able to speak, a situation that is generally denied to almost everyone else. They have found a position within language from which to speak, and the jokes, puns and repartee that seem to flow effortlessly soon follow. We could even explain the famous exaltation of the manic person as exactly an effect of this: mood is elevated because they are able to speak, rather than vice versa. It's not the mood that allows them to speak, but the speaking that liberates the mood. Mania thus involves an apparent paradox. Language has a certain autonomy of its own, with connections branching out from one word to another which unfurl before the manic subject. But at the same time, although they seem to be slave to these racing thoughts, they have a place within language from which to articulate them.

Perhaps this is less of a contradiction than it immediately appears. First of all, note the drift, which starts from the manic subject having a position and ends with them being overwhelmed. Mania, after all, involves a curve, an arc, and is never a homogeneous experience. Then we could ask what, in fact, gives the person a place in speech? If we look at the different forms of flight of ideas, don't they all have one thing in common? Don't they all involve a recognition of the addressee, the one who is being spoken to? Even if the manic subject moves from one topic to the next with an apparent disregard of theme or content, they are still talking *to someone*. When Behrman characterizes mania with the formula 'What would you like to see me do next?', the key is in the 'you'. There is an unquenchable thirst for an addressee. Manic subjects, unlike others, will not talk to themselves.

The pressure here is not simply to speak, but to speak to someone. Studies of manic-depression have indeed sometimes identified the push to relate to others as a central symptom, and, as we have seen, it is telling to observe that this is of course also one of the most dominant social imperatives of our time. Isolation and interiority are discouraged, as we are urged to network, to contact, to connect. There is a cohesion here between what has seemed to many the core of bipolarity and the essence of modern subjectivity. What was once seen as a sign of illness is now identified with a positive norm.

In real mania, however, the push to connect will often go well beyond the conventions of communication. It is remarkable how often in the memoirs of manic-depressive subjects there is a sudden and knowing address to the reader, as if the narrative can and must be broken by a direct appeal to the addressee. This is like the moment in Michael Haneke's film *Funny Games*, when one of the men who has terrorized an innocent family suddenly turns to speak directly to the camera. Such devices can be understood as a postmodern flaunting of narrative conventions, but can't we also see in them an echo of this necessity for some subjects of appealing to their audience, to confirm a complicity and a connection? When the actress Vivien Leigh, caught in an acute manic episode, turned to address the theatre audience directly when playing in *Tovarich*, we see the same need for an addressee, to create and affirm a connection with them.

As Patty Duke writes, at such moments 'the ability to feel what other people feel is almost mystical. It is a mental, spiritual, and physical, indeed chemical, communion of people. I have the sensation that I've sent something out there into the audience and I feel this wave coming back. It really is an energy. It's an actual thing. If you had special cameras, you could probably take a picture of it . . . It's a thrill when I send it out there and they get it. And we share this one infinitesimal moment of unity.' This won't come from interaction with other players in a movie or stage play, but from the moment of impact with the audience itself, the moment when an effect can be created in someone else, one that is not scripted or programmed in advance.

Doesn't this also shed light on the curious promiscuity

of many manic subjects? As Terri Cheney points out, 'manic sex isn't really intercourse. It's discourse, just another way to ease the insatiable need for contact and communication. In place of words, I spoke with my skin.' Sex keeps the addressee right there, up close: the subject moves from one lover to another as they would move from one conversation partner to another. Cheney brilliantly observes that the famous hyperactivity of mania, the constant jiggling, tapping and fidgeting, are simply forms of the pressure to speak, to keep on talking.

The need for the addressee's presence might seem paradoxical, since their own views and opinions tend to be ignored or talked over. Yet this apparent impatience is a clue in itself. Students of manic speech have always been struck by the appeal to so-called 'adventitious stimuli', the sudden reference to random details of some aspect of the environment. Details of a business scheme swerve to a comment about the listener's brooch or the colour of an adjacent chair. Such semantic leaps have been interpreted in a number of ways – a breakdown of associative pathways, the absence of a guiding idea, some innate distractibility – but isn't their most obvious feature the fact that they keep speech going and hence deprive the listener of a chance to respond?

Focusing exclusively on the links between the manic person's words has meant a neglect of this crucial dimension of their effect on the addressee. The leaps involve an excision of the points of suspension in speech, which are exactly those moments that give the other person a space to reply. Manic discourse, however, freezes the listener, and the moment of their response, or the silence that would precede it, is kept at bay. Speaking keeps the other person there, but in this very specific way that has the effect of disarming them. Words exercise their magic – for a time – fixing an addressee and preventing them from any real reply, the kind that could risk dropping or chastising the manic subject. No wonder that the listener, as well as feeling exhausted, will often feel manipulated or controlled.

This is exactly what distinguishes manic-depression from other forms of psychosis, where the person may construct a virtual, distant or internal addressee. There has to be a real listener right there in front of them. And yet there is something tenuous, desperate even, about how the manic person maintains their interlocutor, as if they had to have them there at all costs, like a nightclub entertainer who has to keep his audience focused on himself at all times. Is it an accident that manic-depression is so common in the world of comedians?

As Freud saw, to study mania means thinking about how jokes work. The explosion into punning and wit described so frequently by manic subjects shows how a bond with another person is created through words. When we tell a joke or employ wit, it is usually in situations of unease or threat. Alone and isolated with another person, what better tool do we have to win them over or to make them less threatening?

Jokes unite and bond, creating a connection between two people generally at the expense of a third party, the butt of the joke. They also involve guilt. If we feel guilty about something, perhaps a sexual or a violent thought in ourselves, wrapping it up as wit allows the temporary experience of release, as if we could redistribute the burden that we feel. Isn't that why the most common initial reaction to hearing a joke is first of all the thought of who one will tell it to next? And for the teller of the joke, it is a feeling of relief, of a split-second success, perhaps followed by the warm sensation of being loved. A joke involves the idea of its transmission, of passing it around, whether in person or through an email or phone call.

That's why if you observe the audience during a comedy film, they keep looking not just at the screen but at each other, whereas if it's a tragedy the gaze remains fixed to the screen. Jokes always involve a third party, as if our affect of laughter both depends on someone else laughing and is sanctioned by them. Describing his first manic episode, a businessman explained how 'I found it intoxicating to be able to make people laugh in the office. I could even make people on the tube laugh. Jokes and punchlines just kept coming naturally.'

He felt that he had to make people laugh, as if this were 'almost a duty', and mania is perhaps a way of trying to keep one's audience alive, afloat, to keep an addressee right there in front of you. When this runs into difficulties, we find terrible anxiety and paranoid thoughts start to gather. There is the realization, brought home through frictions and conflicts, that, as the businessman put it, 'no one else is on the same page as you'. The sense of connectedness collapses, and in its place comes the abyss of depression, as if the sense of failure and shame when a joke one tells falls flat had been multiplied ten thousandfold.

—

Holding an audience evokes a very specific aspect of childhood, described by many manic-depressive subjects. A mother, father or other primary caregiver is themselves subject to mood changes, often unheralded and terrifying to the child, who feels dropped and then adored with a ferocious inconsistency. This dramatic see-saw can be a daily experience, or can occur at the time of the birth of a sibling, for example. In some cases, a mother can only remain close to her child if a situation of complete dependency is maintained. The moment the child starts to assert its independence, her love collapses. The pendulum-like structure of some forms of manic-depression is thus literally inscribed on the child.

Such ruptures mean that their most basic experience is to be highly invested and then jettisoned, a pattern that they may later relive in their own mood swings, where they feel either at the centre of the world or unbearably deserted and alone. Similarly, later in life, they may seek relationships of absolute dependency as a way of guaranteeing love. Another person becomes all-powerful to them, a source of every supply, and the tiniest slight or frustration is magnified into a feeling of absolute rejection.

In Terri Cheney's memoir of her childhood she describes the ups and downs of her moods, and calls the affliction she felt inside her the 'Black Beast'. As we read of its invasions and retreats, it is difficult not to see it as almost an exact barometer of her father's pleasure or displeasure in her. This Beast that could make her moods plummet and soar seems to be an embodiment of his interest in her, his passion for her and his disappointment when she failed to live up to his ideals of academic achievement.

Similarly, Kay Redfield Jamison describes her father's manic exuberance, his 'infectious enthusiasm' and the 'contagious magic' of his expansiveness, precisely the qualities of some of her own manic highs. When she was up she would be 'flying high', and one can hardly help but notice that her father, who had been a pilot, would often say to her 'we can fly'. She both 'glides' and 'flies' in a manic episode, singing 'Fly Me to the Moons' [sic] as she moves through the rings of Saturn. Although her father was first of all a scientist, 'his mind and his soul ended up being in the skies'.

The insistence on a genetic basis for manic-depression often obscures this simple logic: a parent or grandparent's manic-depression is used to explain the child's, as if a genetic sequence has been transmitted, rather than crystallized through the actual experience of that child's interactions with them. As Patty Duke put it, her own children 'didn't know what to expect'. Even when things were pleasant enough, 'you just never knew when the good times would be over'. If one is valued and then dropped, this mortifying rhythm may become the parameter of one's own reality, unless something else intervenes to offer another pathway.

We often see this in those whose worldly success seems so assured and incontestable to others. Celebrated actors and comics, from Spencer Tracy to Spike Milligan, would lie awake at night waiting for the phone call or letter announcing their downfall. The studio would drop them, their bank would declare them penniless, their agent would tire of them. Praise, success and admiration would ultimately register far less than criticism and failure, as if the only purpose of an up would be the down that followed.

From this perspective, mania perpetuates the once-fragile sense of connectedness, the one feeling that was so excruciatingly discontinuous for the child. The time of feeling deeply linked to the mother or caregiver becomes the experience of the whole world: now *everything* is linked together, love is everywhere, good vibes and possibilities for the future. When Behrman made his first court appearance for art forgery, he felt that he could bond with each juror one by one. 'I feel powerful enough,' he writes, 'to convince anyone of anything.' A manic person may also repeatedly impose themselves on other people, visiting and phoning to the point of exhaustion, as if their place in the other's affections were guaranteed. As Kraepelin pointed out, they want to play a part in things.

This effort to connect reflects the way that the manic subject may have been swept up in the effusive high of a parent, and it contains both a sense of power and a terrible fragility. Fragile not only because the high would inevitably end and they would lose their place as cherished companion, but also, and equally profoundly, because the enthusiasm and vitality of such moments are less shared experiences than desperate measures to be taken to avoid abandonment. Failing to be swept up would result in exclusion and isolation, as if a tenuous, false emotion were the only thread linking child and parent.

A child in this situation has a choice of 'take it or leave it', where the 'take it' can refer to the high of a manic-depressive mother or, in many cases, that of the father, whose high is appealed to as a protection against the depressive state of the mother. If the child fails to participate, they are painfully left out, and if they join the ride, they know that, in the image evoked by my patient, the rocket will disintegrate. Joyful inclusion always carries this sense of false foundations, and it is interesting that careful observers of mania such as the psychiatrists Wilhelm Griesinger and Henri Ey noted how manic subjects seemed to be playing a part or acting, as if their behaviour were not ultimately grounded in a delusional certainty or conviction.

If the child joins the ride, the connection once felt with the caregiver – Duke's 'moment of unity' – may return in the form of mania. Behrman could say that he would feel as if he had a magic power of attracting people, the manic episode perhaps re-enacting the bond he would have once – however momentarily – enjoyed with his caregiver. For Fry, 'I loved the thrill of knowing that I was carrying hundreds of people with me, that they were surfing on the ebb and flow of my voice.' And when friends, colleagues or newly struck acquaintances of a manic person reflect on what it was like for them, they too will evoke this feeling of being swept up, carried along by the enthusiasm, vitality and persuasiveness of the speaker.

It is perhaps no accident here that the investment of the future is so pronounced, since this is precisely what was so unsure, so unstable and so precarious for the child of the manic-depressive parent. Fry contrasts mania, in which 'you plan for 100 futures', with the 'futureless future' of depression. When Simon asks one of her interviewees whether she ever thought in her mania that she could fly, she replies, 'I never thought I could fly, but I never thought I could fall.'

This belief in one's own powers must naturally seem attractive to those who doubt their own. TV programmes like *Dragons' Den* regularly show investors lose interest in the would-be entrepreneurs who lack self-confidence. But where is the line between grandiosity and commitment? As the anthropologist Emily Martin asks, how could one distinguish so easily between the apparently unwell person who says 'I can change the world' and the apparently sane one who says 'I can build an Internet company and make you rich'?

When *Time* magazine featured publisher Phil Graham on their cover, his entrepreneurial activities seemed elevated to the status of an ideal. Here was someone perpetually busy, buying newspapers and journals, helping to run *Newsweek* and the *Washington Post*, purchasing his own jet and acquiring TV stations. Yet, as his wife, Katharine Graham, describes in her memoir, this acquisitive energy was a manic one, and his ups would have their counterpoint in terrible, oppressive downs that would end some years later in his suicide.

The American TV anchorwoman Jane Pauley documented her own strange transformation from a modest and careful consumer to a big spender, buying a house that she didn't need and trawling shops and malls for endless furnishings and accessories. Along with this came new ideas and projects that she presented excitedly to her agent. 'I had energy, for one thing, and ideas – many ideas. A show. A book. A magazine' – and even her own line of clothing. 'Feelings came shooting in and out at the speed of bullet trains, along with ideas, followed by phone calls that produced action plans.'

The mania here may be spurred by how contemporary culture shapes our self-image. People are encouraged to sell themselves, to broadcast their achievements, and to generate more and more products or derivatives of their identity. A celebrity today may actually be pressured to launch their own clothing line, TV show or perfume. When Pauley tells her agent that her doctors said she had too many ideas, 'he understood, but assured me they were good ideas nonetheless'. We could ask, indeed, how many creative projects get off the ground not in spite but because of someone's mania?

A manic-depressive man described how the TV series he had conceived was finally produced. 'This long-awaited success provoked my first fully-fledged manic episode, though I didn't know what it was at the time. And when a few other ideas of mine got commissioned I set out to convince the senior management of British TV that I had the Midas touch, not realizing that my overconfidence was fuelled by pure mania rather than actual ability.' But is the dividing line really so obvious? As he continued:

'The problem with being manic is that sometimes it *can* work, and in this case the boss of one of the biggest ITV companies fell for my shtick and gave me a high-powered job with a huge salary and expense account.'

Although this post was to end badly, how many careers, we could ask, draw on and absorb manic highs? Receiving a diagnosis of bipolar today frequently means getting a printed fact sheet with the names of those who, it would seem, certainly did have a Midas touch: Alexander the Great, Einstein, Picasso, Mozart, Dickens, Greene, Luther, Lincoln, Proust, Coleridge, Churchill, Balzac, Conrad, Shelley, Kipling and Newton, to name only a few. Brian Adams, rightly sceptical of what he terms 'manic-depression propaganda', asks why such lists invariably focus on names of those who have con- tributed to culture rather than detracted from it, and wonders where the diagnoses have sprung from, given that, in his own case, it took more than twenty years and half a dozen experts to be recognized by psychiatry as manic-depressive himself.

Emphasizing the manic-depressive's public creativity is, of course, also insensitive and stigmatizing to those who do not write or sculpt or paint or conquer to world- wide recognition. Emily Martin reports that at the 2000 meeting of the American Psychiatric Association, a pharmaceuticals company had actually installed a real live artist at the Zyprexa stand, who worked on a collage over several days for conference participants to observe. Strewn in front of his large canvas were paints, glues, fab- rics and fibres, as if to show not only that bipolar subjects can make things but that drugs will not get in the way.

Creativity becomes, at one extreme, a circus exhibit, and at another, a localizable and marketable property of the psyche.

After Brian Adams experienced the usual disappointment at his local Employment Service Assessment and Counselling Centre, he asks, 'What did I expect, a magic wand waved to set me off on some new life-twist in a job where my manic-depression would fit in perfectly?' All the propaganda is hardly helpful here: ' "Well, Mr Adams," ' he writes, ' "we think that after looking at your psychological profile, work experience, life experience, interests, aptitudes, birthmarks, shoe size, the tea leaves, your psychosis and the general cut of your jib, we can confidently put you forward for training as Alexander the Great." '

The well-intentioned propaganda around manic-depression opens up another question. In manic states, people tend to believe that they are powerful, capable and endowed with skills that most people don't have. Among the first questions, indeed, that one of my patients was asked when hospitalized was: 'Do you ever believe you will be a famous artist?' Given that most artists must have entertained such a belief at one time or another, one might imagine that a more appropriate question would be 'Are you a famous artist?' – although in my patient's case this would have been even more confusing as she was, in fact, a famous artist.

Marshalling a list of names of high achievers, from Alexander the Great to Picasso, curiously mirrors the clinical problem of grandiosity that is supposedly to be treated. And this brings us to a crucial aspect of manic-depression. Whereas some psychotic subjects can assert that they are Christ or Napoleon, they are often perfectly happy to carry out menial tasks, such as laundry or kitchen duties. They are very unlikely to present themselves at an ecclesiastical congress or a military barracks. Yet in manic-depression, the person may really book a hotel suite at Claridge's or try to reserve a daily table at The Ivy.

What is happening at the level of identity here? The answer perhaps lies in the comparison of the manias and the depressions. The person sees themselves as worthless and alone in the low phases, and as supremely capable and powerful in the highs. But isn't the key the fact that they *see themselves* as these things, since this supposes an external point of perspective which has been internalized. Their self-image has been constituted from this point, just as Terri Cheney describes the peaks and troughs of her moods as governed by her father's changing perspectives on her.

Many years ago, the psychoanalyst Frieda Fromm-Reichmann and her colleagues had argued that the constellation in manic-depression often involves an aspiration to a better social position, with the child earmarked to achieve this for their family. Coming from backgrounds in minority groups due to their religious, economic or ethnic status, the child is given the task of gaining prestige in an adverse world. 'In this setting,' they write, 'the manic-depressive is very early burdened with the family's expectation that he will do better than his parents in the service of the prestige of the family and clan.'

The child is coerced to conform to impossibly high standards of behaviour, based on how the parent believes 'others' should see them. There is thus a sense of impersonal authority, a 'they', forever evoked in front of the child, who has to win its prestige. The weight of moral and worldly ideals can be crushing here. The son of a mother who had told him that the family's uprooting from one country to another was solely for his own benefit, and that one day he would own the city and that the 'sky is the limit', would later be hospitalized after a manic episode when he believed that his car would take off like a plane.

The maternal ideal could propel him in the mania, but not stabilize him or provide any secure framework for his life. The identity that the child is pressured to assume – willingly or not – is both false and precarious, and we can note the frequency with which manic-depressive subjects are described as obedient and dutiful children, as this suggests again the presence of an ideal that the child conforms to rather than challenges. Fromm-Reichmann's description of social background does not need to be taken literally, but her emphasis on this impact of ideals in manic-depression is spot on. It also sheds light on the fact that depressive lows and manias may ensue not from failures but from social successes. When the child has finally arrived at the point that he was supposed to reach, there can be no real satisfaction, as this was always someone else's ideal.

In Andy Behrman's case, the manic episodes often

involved him getting on a plane to take random flights, or aiming to fly around the world. Although the collapsing of distances is a common feature of manic-depression – where geographical separation seems trifling and everything can seem close by – it is difficult not to link this also to the fact that he was going to be named after an astronaut, the first American 'to orbit the earth', yet whose mission had been delayed on the day of Behrman's birth. 'Growing up, I naturally assumed they had great expectations for me,' he writes, and he would fantasize as a child about circling the planet. In one terrifying episode: 'I felt locked inside a globe, like the one I grew up with, showing all the continents and countries in relief.'

If we move now to another of the motifs of mania, why the shopping sprees and extravagance? A manic person may spend vast sums of money on clothes, property, artwork or objects that they may later look at quizzically in what Brian Adams calls the 'après-mania'. In a TV programme about bankruptcy, a woman was asked how she had managed to get through her City salary and end up in terrible debt. What had she spent it on – holidays, cars, homes? asked the interviewer. No, she replied bashfully, she liked 'those large prawns'. This could be understood as a trope for a luxurious lifestyle, but if the person is manic-depressive, the reference may be absolutely literal. Fortunes can be squandered on what seem to others like idiosyncrasies. Spending money that one doesn't have is such a common feature of manic states that initiatives have been launched by the finance industry to help the manic subject negotiate their way through post-episode debt.

These sprees are sometimes described as selfish, narcissistic rampages showing no regard for family or friends, who often have to pick up the bill afterwards. Yet the more we listen to accounts of what has happened, the more we realize that there is a certain altruism, a sacrificial logic at play in the sprees, and indeed, a manic subject can just as well give away possessions as acquire new ones. Vivien Leigh would have to be kept away from fancy stores like Cartier and Asprey during her episodes, yet her spending would so often involve buying gifts for the cast and crew of the productions she was acting in. Acquiring and giving away are equated here. The Wall Street trader John Mulheren Jr, speaking about his experience of manic-depression, described how he would put twenty thousand dollars in envelopes and hand them out to underprivileged people in the Bowery, a poor district of Manhattan.

One of my patients, zigzagging round London during a manic episode, heard the troubled tale of a minicab driver, and, redirecting the car to his bank, gave him his life savings there and then 'out of compassion'. For Lizzie Simon, 'It feels so right to do something for someone, something you wish someone had done for you. So right it's completely intoxicating.' To take another example, a man visited me for a first consultation in a manic state. When I opened the door, he immediately handed me a cheque, informing me that he had to dash off to meet someone so couldn't stay, but here was the fee, which, as he found too low, he had multiplied by ten. I never saw him again, but his wife phoned not long afterwards to make sure I never cashed the cheque.

The projects undertaken by a manic person are often directly related to helping others, the righting of wrongs, or some act of protection. Kay Redfield Jamison reports her purchase of several snakebite kits, with the idea that she had been chosen to alert the world to the proliferation of killer snakes in the San Fernando Valley. In buying the kits, she says, 'I was doing all I could to protect myself and those I cared about.' When she was beset by thoughts of 'the slow painful death of all the green plants in the world', she notes that as they died one after the other, 'I could do nothing to save them.' One of my patients would spend considerable sums of money helping others, fostering their projects with such energy and enthusiasm that he almost never remembered to take the precautions necessary in any business venture. And Spike Milligan was celebrated for his work with charities trying to protect the world's endangered wildlife.

Manic sprees always need to be explored carefully, as beyond the apparently selfish activity this altruism may be the real motor of the spending. Another patient described how she would go from shop to shop, spending thousands on outfits that would then remain confined in bags and boxes. Were they items she had coveted and only when manic allowed herself to purchase? Not at all, she explained, they were like uniforms, 'the costumes for people I could be'. Yet these were the costumes she imagined the man she had made so central to her life would like to see her in: 'they were objects that conjured up the potential of what I could be for him'. After the sprees, she said, 'I'm always left with a wardrobe of unactivated props.'

These props were there as part of a theatre designed less for her than for Him, as if she were playing out characters from his fantasy. The spending was thus indexed less to herself than the image she would create for someone else, as if, once again, an ideal was governing her actions, an ideal that shaped both her behaviour and her appearance. The external aspect of this control is evoked in another description of the manic spending sprees: 'It's like watching someone else take control of your life.' There is almost literally someone else there.

When Stephen Fry donned elaborate suits and drank cocktails at the Ritz and the Savoy during his first manic episode, he undertook what he called 'a fantastic reinvention of myself'. Fry describes this reinvention precisely: 'Not only was I a seventeen-year-old trying to look like a compound of Wilde, Coward, Fitzgerald and Firbank, I was a seventeen-year-old in a Gatsby-style suit and starched wing collar smoking coloured cigarettes through an amber cigarette holder.' But where had these collars come from? They were in fact a legacy from his beloved maternal grandfather, Martin Neumann, a Hungarian Jew with a passion for all things English: the very image that Fry would appropriate in these moments.

Just as this reinvention was paid for using stolen credit cards, we can wonder whether the image he created was not linked to someone else's fantasy. His grandfather, after all, had also longed to be an English gentleman. As the protagonist of Fry's first novel puts it, he 'doesn't exist except in borrowed clothes'. The apparent selfishness of the thefts that were funding the spree would thus cover over a deeper and perhaps unconscious altruism or, at least, an identification. Years later, when visiting the house where his grandparents had lived for a television programme, he would position himself exactly where his grandfather had once stood for a photo holding his daughter – Fry's mother. As he maps himself into his grandfather's place, Fry remarks that this is a 'Freudian nightmare'.

We could also think here of the large tips that manic subjects almost invariably leave in bars or restaurants. Is it to create an enlarged image of the self, to make oneself more valued and loveable, or, on the contrary, to give something back to the other, to repay, perhaps, another kind of debt?

We should not underestimate this interpersonal dimension in manic-depression. However egotistical the person's actions may seem, there is always someone else there on the horizon. It has often been observed how the manic person tries to sweep other people up into some scheme or project, frequently with success. This is less about some private enterprise or solitary pursuit than a larger, more encompassing endeavour, perhaps with a social good as its goal. Colleagues, friends and investors may be approached, and real things can and do happen.

Sometimes there is a lack of commitment to one project, and after a few hours or days another one is embarked upon. But there can be a sustained and serious focus, whether the enterprise seems plausible or bizarre to others. One of my patients had once worked for Jaguar, and it struck him during a meeting that the key to success in a certain market would be to replace the famous and familiar logo with that of another jungle animal. He could look back on this with a smile many years later, but at the time it was an absolute conviction: he knew that this was the right thing to do, and he just had to persuade the senior management to open their minds.

What was crucial to him during the manic episode was to guarantee other people's belief in him, and this is perhaps linked to another strange phenomenon we find with quite extraordinary frequency in manic-depression. Many of my patients have compared their experience at certain times to the film *The Truman Show*, where a character lives in an artificial world, broadcast as a reality TV show. They describe the world around them as an artificial construct like a theatre or film set, designed to test or to study them. 'It's a feeling of being a part of something, being part of a bigger picture,' as one man put it after his mania had calmed. 'Life was a game or a test.'

Although a comparable idea of reality can be found in schizophrenia, what is fascinating here is that this 'Truman Show' in manic-depression is always benign. 'No one is who they seem to be, but this is exciting. They are testing me, moving to an even higher level, we're proving ourselves, passing tests, like a game that we're cracking.' In other forms of psychosis, the person may constantly feel that they are being tricked by those around them, but this is largely absent during mania. Yet if reality were a stage-managed set-up, surely one would expect it to be menacing?

Doesn't this give us another clue to manic-depression? The altruism, the sacrificial logic and the benign nature of the observing world all suggest that, for the manic-depressive subject, the belief in a good Other, in a giving and generous world, has to be preserved at all costs. 'It's about goodness,' as a manic-depressive friend put it. 'It's angels rather than demons.' Nothing can taint the beatific vision, and if anything does, they move on quickly, convinced of the fundamental goodness and harmony of their reality.

If in schizophrenia there is the idea that everything is being stage-managed, the agency responsible for this doesn't want the person to know it's a trick. But for the manic-depressive, they're all in it together: they know that we know, in a curious and almost comforting complicity. Likewise, in schizophrenia, the surrounding world can become threatening or persecutory, moving from good to bad with swiftness and terror. Yet for the manic-depressive, this passage is not so easy, and it is blocked by what manic-depression is. The hyphen in the term itself embodies what the condition tries to do: create a separation between two states. Good and bad have to be kept apart at all costs.

Let's take the example of Kay Redfield Jamison once again, whose writings on manic-depression have been so influential. Right at the start of her memoir, *An Unquiet Mind*, she pinpoints what would become perhaps the formative moment of her childhood. She is playing outside, when a jet at the military base where they are living starts to spin out of control. The pilot could have ejected and saved himself, yet instead chose to steer his jet so that it crashed beyond the playground where Jamison and other children were playing. This scene returned to haunt her again and again, and although it certainly presents what might be interpreted as a child's first encounter with death, doesn't it also show exactly the motif of sacrifice that we have been discussing?

The pilot gave up his own life to save others, 'transformed into a scorchingly vivid completely impossible ideal for what was meant by the concept of duty'. The episode fuses the image of altruism, an ideal and a sacrifice. Violence to a child was avoided, and, if we push a bit further, we could guess that the underlying idea is to protect someone else from one's own destructive tendencies or, at least, from a collapse that could also be self-engineered. As Melanie Klein argued, if the terror of the schizophrenic is the falling apart of their own self, for the manic-depressive it is the falling apart of their Other. Old psychiatry, indeed, had noted the wariness of manic-depressive subjects to harm others, even if provoked. When Patty Duke threw plates at her children during a manic episode, her aim was always just good enough to know how to miss them.

As one of the psychoanalyst Edith Jacobson's manic patients explained to her, even though she devoured everything, nothing *happened* to anybody or anything: they were still safe. The central concern here is damage to one's objects. We should pause, however, to nuance the idea of destructive wishes. That a child experiences rage towards and hatred of a parent whom they love is undeniable. Yet is this really the root of such motifs in manic-depression? A patient who had been hospitalized several times for manic episodes explained to me that in her early life she had felt like a 'puppet' for her mother, doing her bidding and being terrified of any condemnation or blame. She often imagined her mother's death, yet less as the enactment of a revenge than as the only form of release. 'I could only be me,' she said, 'if Mum were to die.' This thought would then generate a powerful and ravaging guilt, and produce behaviour designed to please or placate her mother.

Her later manias would aim to protect other people or aspects of the environment. The death wish against the mother was thus not really a vector of hatred but the logical condition of her own emancipation. Another manic-depressive person described how, as his mania gathered momentum, he would be moved by small acts of kindness: 'I'd go out to help people.' He explained how he had become 'expert at identifying with other people', with their pain. As Terri Cheney notes, in mania, even when she was drinking a glass of wine, her heart went out to the poor grapes that had been crushed to make it. The world's lack suddenly opens up, and every passer-by can seem like a well of sadness. Eugen Bleuler reports a case where the patient was so moved by the plight of a solitary bug he noticed on the pavement that he went to a bakery and bought a large trifle, in order to let the poor creature loose in it.

The arc in mania includes this aim to protect another person, which can then extend to charitable or benevolent acts and projects, such as animal welfare or environmental preservation. When Spike Milligan saw the famous Elfin Oak, a 900-year-old tree in Kensington

Gardens that had fairies carved into it by the sculptor Ivor Innes, he was concerned to see how the carvings were now chipped and peeling. Norma Farnes describes how he recruited a team of helpers, persuaded Rentokil to preserve the tree and British Paints to supply the waterproof paint as part of his rescue mission.

Proud of the success of this restoration, he took Farnes to see the tree in its new glory. Only yards from the oak, 'his face moved from horror to ineffable sadness'. Part of one of the carved fairy wings had been snapped off. Returning to his office, Milligan locked himself in for three days and nights, communicating with no one, refusing food, overwhelmed with unbearable despair. When he eventually emerged and Farnes questioned him about the depression, Milligan evoked all the care that had gone into restoring the tree, only to have someone snap off the wing. 'I just want to write scripts and books, poetry and music, to make the world a better place.'

This chimes with another peculiar feature of manic-depression. Whereas today if a manic-depressive person complains of developing obsessive symptomology they are likely to be given a new medication such as clomipramine to remove it, old psychiatry noticed that obsessive symptoms were actually a positive sign. They would frequently develop during the intervals between phases, and consist of doubts – 'Have I turned the tap off? – and different kinds of ordering activity.

This is interesting, as obsessive symptoms can be

understood as ways of avoiding harm to others, minimal treatments of one's own destructive tendencies. Recognizing the coexistence of love and hate, after all, is a terrifying proposition. As Patty Duke puts it, 'it's hard to imagine that you're mad at your mother, that you hate your mother'. If we hate and love, doesn't that mean that we risk losing the other's love due, precisely, to our hate?

The hatred here is so destructive not just because the object is under threat, but because of this momentous risk. Whereas early studies of ambivalent feelings tended to stress the quantitive factor – how much hatred there was – they missed the crucial fact that hatred matters most when it conflicts with an ideal. A child who lashes out at a parent or strikes a sibling may feel guilty and angry with themselves only when they register that violent behaviour means that they lose the ideal image they wish to hold for a parent, and hence risk losing their love.

Freud's patient the Rat Man was overwhelmed by compulsive actions and rituals, such as removing a stone from the side of the road, for fear a passer-by might trip on it, and then returning it from road to pavement for fear that his beloved's carriage might stumble against it. Each part of the ritual of removing and then returning the stone thus aimed to avoid some harm done to another person, yet the very oscillation contained both the crime and its erasure.

Such compulsions are often unnoticeable as they fade into character traits. Theodor Reik describes a patient who was tortured with anxiety about doing some harm to his young son. It had started when he wondered one day whether he had banged the boy's head with a doorknob as he'd entered a room. He then took precautions to make sure nothing like that could ever happen again, yet worried what his friends would think if they saw him in the middle of a sentence elevate his arm to measure the exact distance to the door. So he began to speak in an animated way, throwing his arms out in expansive gestures, pointing at adjacent objects or spreading his arms in a burlesque of extravagant feeling. These gestures were in fact covert measuring devices: the new radiance was in fact the disguise of hostile wishes and his protection against them.

Obsessive symptomology with its procrastinations, rituals and doubts shows that the proximity between love and hate, between preservation and annihilation, cannot be adequately resolved. Unable to choose, the person constructs symptoms that maintain conflict in a kind of stasis, with the hostile wishes generally kept outside consciousness yet returning in the compulsive rituals and thoughts. The oversolicitousness of the obsessional both conceals and carries the vector of destruction.

Manic-depression involves a more extreme separation of love and hate, and the effort to avoid harm coming to those we love – or a denial of our responsibility – perhaps underlies the manic episode. Is it an accident that the two volumes of Stephen Fry's memoirs each open with an allusion to a reparative gesture? The first line of *The Fry Chronicles* is 'I really must stop saying sorry; it doesn't make things any better or worse.' In *Moab is My Washpot*, we read right at the start a curious story about Fry's protection of a little boy called Bunce whom he meets on the train to his boarding school. And the Acknowledgements at the end of the book close with the apology '. . . I can only say Sorry and Thank You.'

Fry's superb books can help us here to understand more about the questions of sacrifice, reparation and debt in manic-depression. He writes early on in *Moab* of his addiction to sugar, starting with a childhood passion for the cereal Sugar Puffs. 'The breakfast table is where the seeds of my sorrow were sown. I am sure that I am right in locating my first addiction here' – an addiction that would move from cereal to sweets to cocaine. Fry's grandfather was an expert on the cultivation of sugar beet, and when the prospect of another war seemed probable, with the closure of sea routes from the West Indies and Australia, the British government invited him to oversee domestic production. He moved from his Hungarian home town of Surany – absorbed into Czechoslovakia in 1920 – to Bury St Edmonds in Suffolk. The relocation saved his life: Neumann's family who remained in Surany were wiped out by the Nazis.

As Fry says, 'I should never have been born if it weren't for sugar, and yet it came close to killing me too.' Sugar 'gave me life, but it exacted a price – slavish adherence. Addiction to it and an addiction to addiction in addition.' The taste for cereals moved to sweets at school, and he would steal money to fund their purchase at the village sweet shop, a place forbidden to the schoolboys. Fry was fascinated and enraptured by the new world that the confectionery opened up to him: 'the extra sugariness of the sweets, the blindingly bright cheerfulness of the wrappers', which included liquorice pipes and coconut tobacco, elements that would coalesce in his later passion for smoking and the image of the pipe-toting Sherlock Holmes. As Fry observes, 'All the elements were now in place. Sugar. White Powder. Tobacco. Desire. Lack of money. The forbidden.'

Describing later his problem with limits, Fry notes that 'Where Pinocchio had Jiminy Cricket I had my Hungarian grandfather. He had died when I was ten, and ever since the day of his going I have been uncomfortably aware that he was looking down and grieving over what the Book of Common Prayer would call my manifold sins and wickedness.' If this grandfather watched him 'steal, lie and cheat', this was a gaze that could not stop him from the pursuit of his crimes perhaps for the simple reason that it was inconsistent. Fry quotes his grandfather as saying that a Hungarian Jew is the only person who can go into a revolving door behind another man yet come out in front of him, an aphorism that is put into the mouth of a character in all but one of Fry's novels.

If the relationship with his grandfather was crucial, what can it tell us about manic-depression as such? The chain Fry traces is absolutely convincing: sugar – cereal – sweets – stealing – white powder, used, he tells us, not to enhance but to dampen his highs. We could note that the cereal he chose was indeed the only one to actually have the word 'sugar' in it – Sugar Puffs – and that it is perhaps not coincidental that Fry evokes its iconic Jeremy Bear, when, years later, this very busy personality would find the time to make two television programmes about bears in Peru. Similarly, Fry, well known for his infatuation with Mac computers, tells us that 'Granddaddy was watching, that I knew. It was the one great worm in every delicious apple I ever stole.'

Now, Fry describes how he reinvented himself in his first manic episode, and it would be prudish not to recognize here the identification with his grandfather. Even decades later, on *The Jonathan Ross Show*, he uses the same phrase, telling the TV presenter that he – Ross – had 'reinvented' himself, and that he was 'happy to see an old man come back again'. Just as Fry's grandfather had loved all things English, playing the 'Englishman' in games as a child and donning plus fours and tweeds whenever possible, so Fry remarks of himself, 'I just seem to be made of tweed', noting the irony that he, a Hungarian Jew, should come to embody and represent Englishness itself.

But what could the context be of this identification? Everyone, after all, has deep-rooted identifications with family members. Doesn't Fry make it clear when he says that he owes his life to sugar: that without sugar he would not have existed? The overarching framework of his existence is a debt. We can remember here that the word 'mania' comes from the Greek μανία, a term usually translated as 'madness' or 'frenzy', yet which in plural form evoked the spirits identified by Pausanias with the Eumenides, whose function it was to pursue those who had not, precisely, paid their dues.

———

The fact that manic subjects quite literally create huge debts before the very eyes of their family and friends thus takes on a new sense. The person is showing directly that they are in debt, and the altruistic, sacrificial side of the manic episode may be the attempt to repay this or, alternatively, to cancel it out. The key here is that the manic subject is not aware of any sense of debt until after the episode. Taking this seriously means that the effort to repay the person's empirical financial debts for them might, in many cases, only reignite the original cycle.

A patient of the psychoanalyst Abraham Brill described his manic high in terms of exactly this cancellation: 'I became very buoyant. All sense of responsibility seemed to leave me, and I felt very free and happy. All my life I have felt constrained, tied down, enslaved by conditions and circumstances, and now I seemed reborn into another life, another world in which people were very different from what they were before.'

Brill's example is particularly illuminating as this patient had in fact been held responsible for the death of his younger brother as a child. Their sister had been trying to fry an egg in the hearth, a fire had started, and the boy died in the blaze. The mother had blamed Brill's patient for not having stayed at home with his brother, and for not having taken him along with him when he went out. The mania had triggered after a work accident in which his arm had been crushed, and would later have to be amputated. As he looked down at the limp limb and mangled fingers he had the thought 'That fellow is pretty badly smashed up.' Before the mania itself began, he experienced an odd dissociation: 'My mind was myself and the hurt fellow was like a weak brother that in some way I was partly responsible for.'

This question of responsibility may lie behind the

more immediate motifs of hostility and destruction that we find in manic-depression. If there is an effort to protect the Other from one's own violence and to keep them safe, isn't there also a problem of responsibility that moves between the parties? Fry owes his life to sugar and to the grandfather who escaped the Nazis, but what about the latter's own debt to those he could not save and who were left behind? With Jamison, the pilot's act of sacrifice created a debt in those he had saved, one which may also have evoked a question about responsibility for a death further back in her own family history.

In case after case, we find a dilemma about responsibility at the level of preceding generations. It is often the parent of the manic-depressive person who will have experienced the tragic loss of a child, a sibling or a parent, and the responsibility for this death remains unresolved. In her depressed phases a woman would google endlessly to find images of deformed babies, and ruminate over all the things she had done wrong in her life. The idea that others would think badly of her was unbearable. When manic, she felt intensely powerful, and would help aspiring professionals in her field of work to start their businesses.

Her manias would trigger at the moments when the products she designed were launched, the moments when 'I brought something into the world'. As a child, she had overheard a conversation in which she had learned that her mother had miscarried a baby, described as 'just arms and legs mixed up'. We could note how when high she would help those she thought of as children, yet in the lows her preoccupation with images of deformed babies was never linked consciously to her broodings over the bad things she had done. The question of responsibility for the death could not be directly posed for her, just as it could not for her mother, who otherwise blamed her daughter for everything.

Clinicians working with manic-depression have at times argued that there is always a preoccupation with death in their patients, but it is less death as such than the question of the responsibility for it. This should not be reduced to the death wishes a child might have towards a parent as it involves the parent's own relation to what they have lost. The guilt that cannot be assuaged or inscribed for one generation will haunt the next, just as a debt is passed on. But this debt does not get settled. It crystallizes neither as paranoia ('the Other is responsible') nor as melancholia ('I am responsible'), see-sawing instead between the highs and lows of the manic-depressive subject. If responsibility departs in the mania, it returns in the depression.

Doesn't this also help us to explain the curious vacillations around the sense of identity in manic-depression? One of the most frequently voiced questions is whether the 'illness' is some kind of foreign body or in fact an intrinsic part of the self. Would the person really be themselves after the proposed chemical excision of their mania? Do the highs and lows reveal or obscure who they really are? Should manic-depression be seen as constituting or as compromising the self? The remarkable ubiquity of these questions perhaps echoes the underlying uncertainty about a responsibility. Not knowing whether the manias and depressions belong to us or not reflects the difficulty of not knowing whether the responsibility is ours or someone else's. And isn't the most common thought after a manic episode precisely to ask 'What have I done?'

Mania perhaps involves a foreclosure of the conscious feeling of guilt and debt. Seducing her best friend's boyfriend, Cheney felt that 'something was wrong here, terribly wrong, but what that thing was I just couldn't remember. He was gorgeous, I was available, what else mattered?' The debt to her friend was erased in that moment. As Patty Duke put it, 'When you're manic, there are no consequences.' It is striking to hear from manic subjects how horrified they are when reconstructing what they actually did in their mania. Sexual encounters with and propositions made to the spouses or partners of one's best friends seem totally natural at the time, only afterwards taking on their full weight and consequence. Promiscuity in mania is usually seen simply as an example of general disinhibition, yet beyond this, doesn't it show a temporary abolition of the barriers of guilt that regulate social relations?

Vivien Leigh would play a parlour game when high called 'Ways to Kill Babies', in which her guests were invited to mime unusual ways to dispose of an unwanted child. Given her own history – in which there had not only been a stillborn child before her birth but twins after her who did not survive for more than a week, not to mention her detachment from her own daughter and the powerful feelings of being unwanted which she herself grappled with – what could have allowed her to act out such fantasies so blithely? Was it not the idea of a temporary release from debt, from the question of responsibility for a death, which would only immobilize her when it returned later in her depressive phases?

And this brings us to another point. However fascinating it is to find connections between Fry's memoirs and his fictional work, there is little point in attempting a psychobiography for the simple reason that Fry has done this already. For many people, it would take years of analysis to pinpoint the fundamental signifiers of their existence, yet Fry seems to access the chain sugar–sweets–cocaine with astonishing ease. But he does more than this. He also presents incredibly important and significant insights as a kind of joke. Rather than seeing this as mere affectation or modesty, why not link it to the very structure of manic-depression that Fry has so often explored?

This echoes clinical experience. Manic-depressive subjects may arrive at key connections in therapy, which have little or zero effect, as if insight had no real value. Perhaps what has made some clinicians despair of working with manic-depression here is in fact a clue as to its very logic. When manic, the signifiers that determine one's life are just words among other words, as if their full weight has not been registered. They can be cast as mere jokes or flippant comments. The depression is then the return of their weight, the massive impact of which is absent in the times of mania.

This levity with the words that determine our lives – what psychoanalysts call the 'symbolic' – is perhaps the very signature of manic-depressive structure, and explains why such subjects are so often able to find new and surprising links between words. Think, for example, of the extraordinary verbal dexterity of Oscar Wilde, of Fry or of the late Sebastian Horsley. Language can be turned inside out, dazzling analogies and juxtapositions invented and discovered. To be able to do this, there has to be an ability to move around language, to not be weighed down by significations: exactly what is inverted when mania becomes depression. Here the person is crushed beneath one univocal meaning: they are worthless, unloveable, sinful. Where in mania, meaning seems loose and untethered, in depression it is heavy and constricting.

We see this levity of the symbolic in the vignette we evoked earlier of the Jaguar employee who suggested that they change the company logo. Of course, decisions like that can and do happen, sometimes changing the future of companies, but in this instance the salient feature is the way that my patient did not feel constrained to honour the long connection between the logo and the company. They could be separated, prised apart. The weight of the symbolic wasn't felt here. Words themselves can be invested, more than basic significations. But then there is a dreadful price to pay – in the depressive phase. The depressive agony is thus entirely justified, a kind of payback. As the psychoanalyst Edward Glover once remarked, manic-depression is like an alternating hypertrophy and atrophy of 'unconscious conscience'.

The motif of debt illuminates many other phenomena of manic-depression. A journalist explained how his manias attracted little attention as they were absorbed in 'a whirlwind of work'. He would never say no to a request for a piece in his particular field, and was always frantically busy at these times. Although we could see the work as a way of using his manic 'energy' fruitfully, doesn't the systematic acceptance of every commission also show the sense of an unpaid debt? We hear this often from manic-depressive subjects, especially in the media world: although it might go against their professional judgement, they find it difficult to say no to a job, for fear of letting the Other down.

This can perhaps shed light on the strange proximity of spending and stealing in manic highs. We have seen already how sprees tend to be funded with borrowed money, usually with the bailouts coming after the spending itself. The manic subject spends money that in most cases they do not have. But a spree can also take the more modest form of a series of thefts. As Behrman explains, 'Most days I need to be as manic as possible to come as close as I can to destruction, to get a real good high – a $25,000 shopping spree, a four-day drug binge, or a trip around the world. Other days a simple high from a shoplifting excursion at Duane Reade for a toothbrush or a bottle of Tylenol is enough.'

What might spending and stealing have in common? On an immediate level, if the spending takes place with no funds to support it, it might be construed as a form of theft, encouraged indeed by contemporary markets which rely on people spending money that they don't have. At another level, both activities involve taking something from a significant place, some particular department store or boutique. It's as if the person were buying without paying, and manic subjects often describe their sense of a world of bounty, of supplies, a world where things don't run out. Jamison writes that in her manic spending sprees, 'I couldn't worry about money if I tried. So I don't. The money will come from somewhere; I am entitled; God will provide.' Jacobson's patient could say, 'the world is so rich, there's no end to it'. For Duke, in mania, 'we're going to be millionaires, and we believe it'. As one of my patients put it, speaking of cigarettes one day, 'The thing about fags is, there's always more of them.'

In the manic state, the world seems generous and all-forgiving. Everything is there, to be taken and enjoyed. It seems, in fact, as if the person is stripped of their very socio-symbolic framework: religious and economic. Gone is the work ethic peculiar to that person's background, the modesty or inhibition consonant with their culture, and even, at times, the dietary prohibitions of their religion. Their sense of vitality and energy seems proportional to this loss: as they shed the strictures of the forces that have shaped them, they are 'reborn', and the world seems radically new and promising.

But just as the debt to one's background and history can suddenly become light in the manic episode, so it returns with a force in the depressive phase. The person is now so tied down that sometimes they literally cannot move. When Adams's well-intentioned friends told him to get out more, to try going for walks, what they didn't realize was that he couldn't even get past his own front gate, so paralysed was he. If in the manic high the

59

person takes something without paying, now he pays without any doubt. Debt cannot be foreclosed without returning in its lethal, crippling forms.

If in mania the person has the joyous feeling of no longer being judged, of no longer being responsible, now judgement returns in a powerful, shattering way in the depressions. The fact that so many manic-depressive subjects report turning over in their minds all the bad things they have done, even years previously, during their lows, shows how any events from one's life, however trivial, can be recruited to add muscle to the condemnatory judgement. If in mania the person's speech can move from one theme to another with ease and fluency, now in depression words can be limited to just repeating again and again a single phrase: 'I'm a cunt.'

Let's think more about the link between spending and stealing here. A manic-depressive man described how he would go on shoplifting expeditions each time that his expectations were dashed. 'I would feel anger and rage, as if things had been messed up for me. Stealing was like taking revenge.' Note how the accent here is on how things were messed up *for him*, rather than how he might have messed things up *himself*. The stealing had started at school where he had always taken from the other children who had more than he did, the wealthy kids who came from better homes, better families than his own.

The underlying logic suggests that theft was bound up with the very question of his identity: 'If I can't *be* them, I'll *take* from them.' The patient who spoke of her sprees and 'unactivated props' was guided by the same equation. The man she was involved with, and who would end up paying the bills for her spending, belonged to a class and a culture that she had always aspired to, despite the barrier of her own more modest background. If the clothes she bought were images of who she could be for him, at the fancy parties and polo matches she imagined, through the creation of the debt she was also making him pay.

With Behrman, he was working for a New York artist, initially handling his PR and later taking over more and more of the activities of an agent. The artist was successful, confident, rich – qualities that Behrman himself was drawn towards. Soon, he was in league with one of the artist's assistants, faking paintings and selling them off as originals, even signing the works himself. In Stephen Fry's case, his early spree was funded by stolen credit cards, taken from the very English families he had admired and respected. If he donned the insignia of his grandfather in his act of 'reinvention', we should not forget that this was the grandfather who, in Hungary, had been fascinated by all things English, wearing tweed and gravitating towards an image that was at odds with his own Jewish culture. For both Behrman and Fry, we find an echo of the formula 'If I can't be them, I'll take from them.'

The link between spending and stealing can also be looked at from another angle. Both seem to aim at possession, and old psychiatry had often noted the interest of the manic-depressive subject in acquiring things, whether in the form of objects purchased during a spree or those gathered while hospitalized. As Griesinger observed, his patients collected, accumulated and stole. Was it to deny or compensate for some loss they had experienced in the past?

There are certainly many cases where a mania triggers after a loss, and denial has often been seen as the main mechanism. But at the same time, losing someone we love makes us confront both what they were for us and what we were for them. Beyond the obvious motif of denial, there is perhaps the deeper concern with protecting the one we love, even after they have left us or died. They exist for us, after all, psychically even when they are no longer here, and to keep them from harm may explain part of the altruism of mania.

Patty Duke would run all over town in a manic episode, possessed with an urgency to put everything she had from tissues to earrings in safety-deposit boxes. When we notice how often manic-depressive subjects report the overwatering of plants, we might imagine that the same reparative end is at stake: that of keeping something safe. The ubiquitous obsessive phenomena of tidying and ordering can also be seen here as efforts to make sure that things are in the right place, that is, safe from harm.

There is thus a real dilemma in mania of balancing preservation and destruction. Something must be kept safe from one's own rage or from its own self-destructive tendencies. Rather than grappling with the messy, turbulent mixture of love and hate, destruction and admiration, the manic-depressive person opts for a more extreme and ultimately more coherent solution: to separate love and hate categorically, so that one does not contaminate the other. This means, effectively, that the world of the manic-depressive is peopled with devils and angels. It is either copiously full or desperately empty.

As Melanie Klein observed, the effort here is to keep negative and positive traits separate from each other. Could it be that mania is in itself what happens when they get too close? As one manic-depressive subject explained, her manias would trigger when 'something was too bad to think about, a conflict that was too conflicting'. Unable to symbolize the conflicting ideas *as conflict*, they are split apart. That is perhaps why anger and frustration are so important here. 'When there is nothing else left but rage,' said a patient, 'it becomes elation.' For her, the manias were 'distilled rage'. When asked what would precipitate her episodes, she replied immediately, 'When I get angry with someone I like.'

Splitting love and hate can take a variety of forms here. Another patient described how her mother's mood swings were so unbearable that it was easier to think she had not one mother but two. Now that she had one good and one bad mother, she could direct her love to one and her hatred to another. Duke describes the way she would pray to God that her severely depressed mother would come out of her room and 'be the mommy she was last week'.

This idea inflects the rather simplistic conception of the 'world as breast' in manic-depression. It has been argued that manic highs repeat the experience of feeding at the satisfying breast, and depressions that of the frustrating breast. Yet if supplies seem endless in mania and depleted in depression, rather than just see this as the reflection of a milk-giving breast and a dry or absent breast, isn't it the very effort, as Klein noted, to refuse the fact that the breast is both giving and not-giving, both gratifying and frustrating at the same time? It's 'all supply' or 'no supply' rather than 'both all and none'.

———

Manic-depression is the effort to separate, to maintain an elementary differentiation in the place of a more confusing and more painful set of contradictions. And this is perhaps the real sense of bipolar: not the alternation of moods that much contemporary psychiatry is so eager to pathologize but the search for a primary bipolarity, a baseline splitting of traits. When researchers discuss where everyday mood alternations end and bipolarity begins, they miss this crucial point: that manic-depression is precisely about the effort to create extremes, to create a world of opposites. There is thus no sense in trying to find bipolarity in mood swings unless that is what the person themself is trying to do.

What appear to be extremes of behaviour in manic-depression are thus ways of purifying extremes: grey must be separated into black and white. As Terri Cheney says, 'mania doesn't just give you the desire for extremes, it gives you the energy to pursue them'. Binaries must be kept distinct, and bipolarity is less a pendulum of moods than an effort to keep two poles apart. Cheney tells us that mania is more than a 'disease': it is a way of thinking: 'The world should be one way or another . . .' 'Men either made you feel safe, or they made you bleed. If they weren't gods, they were villains . . .'

We can see bipolarity here as a kind of solution. A

patient described the onset of a manic episode after seeing a woman who resembled her mother on the tube reading a book entitled *Angelic Spirits*. This, for her, was a contradiction, since angels were good but she had always thought of her mother as a 'spirit' when the latter was possessed with a malevolent force. 'Angelic Spirits' thus had to be kept apart and fusing them was impossible. The many binary pairs that emerged during the subsequent mania could be seen as ways to keep the two separate.

Another patient described how, when hospitalized, she had 'used symbols' to regain an equilibrium. Sunlight was bad, but the night's blackness was good. She had then used these terms to generate sets, so that all bad things were 'symbolized' by sunlight and all good things by blackness. Now, as she stayed awake throughout the night, good and bad could be kept separate. She would try to sleep at exactly those points when the barriers between light and black were most fluid: at dusk and at sunrise.

We could remember Spike Milligan and the Elfin Oak. Instead of feeling a mixture of sadness and anger, perhaps, at finding the reparative work on the tree tarnished by the fairy's broken wing, he was plunged into a vortex of despair. The bad could not contaminate the good. For Milligan, it was absolute: the two traits had to be kept categorically apart.

This separation can be seen as a way of treating the question of responsibility that we evoked earlier. The broken wing meant that Milligan had failed, and that his debt had not been cancelled. Responsibility now hit him like an express train. It wasn't the fault of vandals or some careless child but his own, and the magnitude of the guilt he felt at that moment suggests it was the vehicle of something else from his or the family's past.

Any situation that involves violence and hate may stir up this motif of responsibility, and hence the importance of protecting the Other from harm. As a patient put it, 'It's not so much the aggression as the fact that people will think it's *my* aggression.' There is a horror of being seen as violent, as if an ideal of pacifism had to be maintained at all costs. Altruistic acts aim to guarantee this ideal, and so any suggestion of hostility or failure can be ravaging. It would confront the person with a responsibility that can never be entirely assumed.

One of the most frequent forms of safeguarding other people here is to idealize them and it is striking to see this echoed in the memoirs of manic-depressive subjects. If one reads works by those who have been labelled 'schizophrenic', there is often a critique of dominant value systems, yet in those of the manic-depressive we find less critique than endorsement. Pages of disappointment with mental health workers and medication will almost invariably be followed by a sentence such as:

'Then I met the best doctor.'
'Then I met the greatest therapist.'
'Then I found the perfect drug.'

Jamison's work, for example, is in many respects a sustained apology for lithium, with an idealization of 'Science' and good doctors. The rollercoaster ride through her experiences always settles into an encomium for some doctor, drug or therapist. Without denying the worth of these agents, it is tempting to guess that it is not simply the doctor or the drug that has helped her but the actual function of idealization itself. It is otherwise quite extraordinary that someone who has met so many professionals, read so many books and had so many encounters with the mental health system can still shelter behind an idea that 'Science' will solve things.

Where schizophrenic subjects will often question power structures, the manic-depressive may invest some person or agency with unimpeachable authority. Fromm-Reichmann and her colleagues pointed out that any therapist working with schizophrenia must respect the patient's need for a degree of 'isolation from, skepticism and independence of conventional values'. With manic-depression, on the contrary, 'the therapist must help them to break through their dependency on their family or its substitutes and to re-evaluate family conventions'. The manic-depressive has not given up their belief in the Other. The emphasis, they argued, should thus be on questioning convention, undermining idealizations of authority that are already operative.

Such idealizations may also function as an artificial form of debt. When Jamison tells us that 'The debt I owe my psychiatrist is beyond description', we could read this quite literally. Idealization can be a way of constructing a debt. If manic-depression revolves around a foreclosure of debt, refashioning a new debt makes sense, especially if it is felt to be such a massive one. The feeling of indebtedness to some authority can sometimes help to stabilize a manic-depression, and it would be hasty to campaign against idealizations without giving due reflection to their function in each individual case.

This may also be linked to the pervasive search for perfection experienced by so many manic-depressive subjects. Faced with the inconsistency of a parent, the terrifying limbo of not knowing whether one will be loved or ignored when one next sees them, the child may construct an ideal of both personal and parental perfection. If personal perfection entails an identification with an ideal image, conforming with how we imagine the parent wants us to be, parental perfection means that the mother or father's own vacillations are negated. With great frequency, this operation is carried out later in life using parental substitutes, so that someone is found to embody a consistent and benevolent gaze: a doctor, a therapist, a friend. Usually this person has a little bit of distance from them, allowing the idealization to be perpetuated. Too much proximity would mean, after all, inevitable disappointment.

When things are going badly, there may be an effort to appeal to this ideal, which could take the form of a perfect man or woman or, at times, the 'perfection' of a home or some object. Duke describes how she would do her best to create the perfect meal or holiday for her family, yet get angrier and angrier when the ideal was compromised. 'I had expectations that everything would be perfect, expectations that could never be realized.' Yet rather than simply being flawed or lacking, it was catastrophic: 'Since the occasion couldn't be what I hoped, it would be shit. So I made it shit.' She would tear down decorations, smash plates or slash into her kitchen counter with a butcher's knife. This would be followed by her efforts to repair, to make perfect again.

———

If mania can be a way of trying to separate good and bad, we have a clue as to what happens when the high starts to recede. With great frequency, the person calms down through a focused form of hatred, often in the form of a paranoid thought. After the joy and enthusiasm of his manic highs, a patient would think with loathing of a man who had wronged him and overturned his business years previously. Although these thoughts were intensely unpleasant, they still grounded him: 'I think of that rat every five minutes,' he would say, constructing revenge fantasies and running through them interminably in his mind.

In another case, a woman with manic episodes described how her thirst for drink and drugs transformed into a murderous fantasy as the high 'went into recession'. At first, she felt aggression towards someone she had dealt with during the day. Then she experienced a yearning for alcohol and drugs, which passed as the evening progressed into scenarios in which she would grind her heel into the face of a woman who she heard had mistreated a cat. It turned out that she had learned of this woman's behaviour more than a year previously, yet it only surfaced now in her revenge fantasy.

It may seem as if these negative thoughts need to be treated in their own right, and indeed, medication is often prescribed to alleviate them, yet it is important to recognize their functional value. However painful they may be, they can protect the person from something far worse. Adams describes his growing obsession with access to a fire escape during the production of a play: 'certain that I was right and everybody else was wrong, it was a cause that I could not let go of no matter what the consequences were to me'. Although it led to a falling out with other members of the team, perhaps its ultimate value was therapeutic.

We could think here also of the many run-ins that Spike Milligan had with institutions, in particular with the store Harrods or with the BBC. 'Don't let the bastards get away with it,' he would say, as he poured energy and time into disputes about the whiteness of white envelopes or larger causes such as saving local trees or endangered species. We should remember that campaign work allows not only 'good' to be done but for an enemy to be constructed: it isn't just fighting for a cause, but fighting against some agency or individual. This new persecutor can help to temper a mania.

Creating persecutors is a solution for the simple reason that it puts 'badness' outside the self, organizing it and separating it from whatever is considered 'good'. Although this can generate all manner of disputes with neighbours, shops or institutions, it can also take on the more banal form of house-cleaning. It would be difficult to find a case of manic-depression where this activity does not have an important place, or, indeed, a memoir in which it is not mentioned. Although this could be interpreted as a reparative act on the mother's body, symbolized by the person's home, shouldn't we also see it as a way of creating an elementary binary, of separating good and bad, dirty and clean, a splitting that would have an effect on the intensity of depressive rage?

Vivien Leigh would often decide that the whole of her country property at Notley had to be spotless, and would engage in a marathon of cleaning and polishing. In New York during a manic episode she began to pick imaginary dirt from a carpet until she was eventually sedated. Behrman would hoover his apartment mercilessly inch by inch, feeling a strange satisfaction when all the dirt and dust had been extracted. And during a hospitalization, Brian Adams would campaign for proper cleaning to be introduced by the healthcare trust's management.

Obsessive symptomology can be seen in a new light here. Cleaning and ordering can certainly be a way of treating doubt, as we saw earlier, but also as a fundamental way of keeping things separate. Just as two traits have to be split apart in mania, so the cleaning can aim to differentiate the clean from the dirty. It is another way of dividing up space and of creating a boundary between two things, so that they do not contaminate each other.

The story of Adams's campaign is a rather tragic proof of the ever-widening abyss between healthcare managers and patients. After a series of letters between the parties, a trust official concludes: 'We feel that on the whole the ward is kept clean to a more than adequate standard. However, I do understand that from the point of view of the consumer this may not always appear to be the case.' How odd, Adams notes, that those apparently suffering from conditions in which their view of reality is deemed faulty should then be told that, indeed, the filthy carpet was only filthy from their point of view, thus reinforcing the very separation between 'reality' and 'fantasy' that their stay in hospital aimed to remedy.

—

If paranoid thoughts sometimes herald the end of a manic episode, and if they can have a protective role, what in the end do they guard against? Jamison speaks of 'an almost arterial level of agony' in her lows, 'a pitiless, unrelenting pain' that in some cases of manic-depression can lead to suicide. We have seen how such lows can be understood as payback, the return of the person's sense of debt felt now in every corner of their mind and in every muscle of their body.

Psychoanalysis has often made the mistake here of compounding melancholia with mania, yet melancholias without mania are rather different from the lows of manic-depression. As Behrman points out, 'Contrary to what most psychiatrists believe, the depression in manic depression is not the same as what unipolar depressives report . . . My depressions were tornadolike – fast-paced episodes that brought me into dark rages of terror.' This difference is perhaps reflected in the fact that the term 'manic-melancholic psychosis', although used in the late nineteenth century, was never to gain currency, as if there were a registration at some level that there was not a simple equation between melancholia and the kinds of depression at stake here.

For Jamison, her depressions were spiked with 'periods of frenetic and horrible restlessness'. Her thoughts would be 'drenched in awful sounds and images of decay and dying'. The 'deathful quality' of the images of smoke and flames from the plane crash she had witnessed as a child were always there, 'somehow laced into the beauty and vitality of life'. Her mind would turn relentlessly to the subject of death. 'I was going to die, what difference did anything make? Life's run was only a short and meaningless one, why live?' Exhausted, she could barely get out of bed in the mornings. She describes how she 'dragged exhausted mind and body around a local cemetery, ruminating about how long each of its inhabitants had lived before the final moment'. 'Everything was a reminder that everything ended at the charnel house.' For Milligan,

> The pain is too much
> A thousand grim winters
>   grow in my head
> In my ears
>   the sound of the
>   coming dead.

The accent here is on the transitory and meaningless character of our lives. Human endeavour and achievement are nothing, as we will all turn to dust. The brilliance of life dims suddenly when the spectre of mortality invades the manic-depressive's thoughts. This is quite different to the melancholic's depression, which revolves around ideas of moral, spiritual or bodily ruin. In melancholia, the person rages against themself, broadcasting a litany of self-reproach and complaining without respite of some sin or fault they are guilty of.

A sense of guilt is obviously present in manic-depression, but something is different as well. Where the melancholic can complain of being ruined or destroyed, he ascribes the destructive process to himself, whereas the manic-depressive will also ascribe this outside the self. It's the difference between 'I've destroyed the Other' and 'the Other has destroyed me'. Although the ideas of worthlessness and ruin may be present in both, the emphasis is different. Likewise, whereas the melancholic often feels guilty of some act that has occurred in the past, it is interesting that the manic-depressive subject frequently situates the catastrophe in the future. Something terrible is going to happen.

And where the manic-depressive person may feel worthless and despicable, there is less fixity in the self-reproach and less of an insistence on telling the world. These features are crucial to allow a proper diagnosis of manic-depression, and to distinguish it from melancholia. Where in melancholia the person has taken the fault on to their own shoulders, resolute in their self-abasement and castigation, in manic-depression the fault *oscillates*. In the lows, the person runs through not only their own faults and bad performances but also those of others, and the many ways in which others have wronged them. Hence the common revenge fantasies of the manic-depressive, absent in melancholia. In her terrible depressions, Patty Duke would both chastise herself *and* hold others responsible: 'My thoughts would vary from blaming others to wishing for the absolutely unattainable peace of mind.' It is as if rage cannot be entirely absorbed by guilt, since guilt does not attain the delusional fixity it has in melancholia.

Another difference is important here. The manic-depressive subject may often feel paralysed during a low, as if even the simplest everyday decision could not be taken. Once they've got out of bed, what clothes should they wear, what should they eat, which direction should they walk in, what words should they utter when someone greets them? Whereas in mania, decisions just seem to make themselves, in the depressive state everything freezes, as decisions turn into insurmountable tasks. 'It wasn't that I couldn't decide,' as one patient said, 'There was just no "I" any more *to* decide.'

If the 'I' is treated like a noxious object in melancholic depression, and is thus very much present, here it is rubbed out. 'I felt like I'd lost myself,' one man explained. 'I just wanted to lie still, withdraw from the physical world.' A woman described how she 'just wanted to lie there. I just stopped, as if there was a hole in the middle of my soul.' Vivien Leigh felt in her worst lows as if she were 'like a thing, an amoeba, at the bottom of the sea'. It is difficult not to imagine the attraction of the intense sense of identity felt during mania when contrasted with this void.

If the depressions here are paralysing, they are not necessarily slow. The crackling, fast-paced depressions experienced by many manic-depressive subjects perhaps suggest how the separation of traits, which we have argued is an aim of manic-depression, is unworkable. The term 'manic-depression' is once again suggestive: the depression itself can be manic. There is of course a great clinical variety here, but the simple pendulum model, which involves a swing from one state to another, should be questioned, as many manic-depressives have pointed out. Early-twentieth-century psychiatry in fact noted how so-called 'mixed states', in which there seems to be an amalgam of mania and depression, were perhaps even more frequent than pure mania or depressive lows. Feelings can change from ecstasy to despair in a matter of seconds.

One man described his mixed states as 'like a CD skipping'. Unable to sit down for more than thirty seconds, he felt an acute and ravaging sense of frustration. 'This is worse than any depression,' he continued. 'You can't say that you are either happy or sad.' We could note here how the horror of mixed states is identified with the failure of a binary: neither happy nor sad, indicating once again how the production of contrasts, of splitting, may be what manic-depression aims for as a solution. As another manic-depressive person put it, this time finding a binary: 'The ups are not that happy, and, in fact, "up" and "down" aren't the right words. It's more like "fast" and "slow".'

Jane Pauley describes how her 'mood tides' would be 'sweeping in both directions at once' in such states. 'It felt like a miniature motocross race going on in my head.' Jamison describes the intense fusions of 'black moods and high passions'. She rightly questions the rigid separation of mania and depression, writing that 'this polarization of two clinical states flies in the face of everything that we know about the cauldronous, fluctuating nature of manic-depressive illness', and the possibility that mania is simply an extreme form of depression, an idea broached first by Freud's students. Kraepelin, indeed, whose work served to popularize the notion of manic-depressive 'insanity', could conclude that it would be incorrect to say that a person is either manic or depressed. Their delineation is 'wholly artificial and arbitrary'.

Our argument in fact suggests that if manic-depression is an effort to separate out and differentiate polarities, then mixed states could be seen as the original, basic psychical state rather than as some sort of pathological by-product. The rigid separation evoked by Jamison may be precisely what the manic-depressive subject searches for yet in most cases fails to create. Cheney brilliantly describes the experience of mixed states here: 'I was full of restless, undissipated energy that had no place to go, making me want to strike out and break something, preferably something that would crash and tinkle into a thousand satisfying tiny pieces.' There was all the energy of mania here, but not the euphoria. She felt the desperate need to hit something, but when she did in fact strike the man she was with at the time, she regretted it instantly: she had to hit something, but 'I never meant it to be you.'

The only thing to give Cheney some sense of relief was the sound of breaking glass or china, and she would smash teacups one after the other. 'Few things,' she writes, 'are strong enough to survive that deadly clash of mania and depression. Certainly not love. Love is far too fragile: it is a picture window, just begging to be shattered.' We could link this passage to a memory in her second book when, devastated that her father had chosen her mother instead of her for a dinner out, she smashed a full-length mirror. Glass shards flew everywhere, and in this moment Cheney knew that she had 'murdered my mother's voice', the voice that said No to her accompanying them.

Her mania here was perhaps a form of exclusion of her mother, but what is so striking in Cheney's account is the fragility of love. Mania is often accompanied by a sense of pervasive, universal love, yet now it is described as a mere 'picture window', waiting to be smashed. We know from Cheney's memoir that her manic highs involved an identification with her energized, ebullient father. Being swept up in his schemes was a pivotal part of her childhood, and we have the sense that her enthusiasms were a way of creating a distance from her mother. The love for her father was based on these fragile shared highs, vital to allow an escape from the other parent yet at the same time doomed to disintegrate, like the space shuttle evoked by my patient.

The more fragile the love, the greater, perhaps, the need to invest in it. And this may be a part of the extraordinary sense of loyalty that we find in manic-depression. However they may be mistreated, wronged or maligned by some significant individual, they remain faithful, even if others in their entourage might be dropped for some much lesser evil. Just as they had clung to a love that saved them from a perilous and terrifying space where they could be abandoned at any moment, so they desperately try to ensure that there is one figure who embodies this for them, be it a lover, a doctor or a therapist.

We could note here how separating two traits, which get too close in mixed states, may seem like the right psychical solution, but in fact cannot succeed. Why? Because, as both Klein and Lacan saw, to establish a certain peace in the psyche, two needs to move to three, a dialectical transformation which will almost invariably produce the effect of sadness. Remaining in a field with two terms, the person has little choice but to oscillate between them. With three, a signification can be produced, and a loss situated or triangulated in that person's life.

During a manic episode a woman used her energy to meticulously document the movement of her thoughts. As well as many pages of text, she made a diagram of her manic-depression, a globe with 'suicide' written at the top and 'murder' at the bottom. At the equator, there was a thin line of safe space, yet true safety could be achieved only by bringing together the two poles and the core: 'All three need to come together,' she said, 'but I could never figure that problem out.' She would then spend hours attempting to fit three distinct facial expressions on to the image of a single face, without resolution. Manic-depression, she said, 'is about trying to work out a conflict', to keep two states separate, which is ultimately not possible without some form of mediation by a third.

Let's turn now to one last question: the cyclicity of manic-depression. It is telling here that even the most psychologically inclined investigators have pointed to an underlying biological bedrock. The psychiatrist Harry Stack Sullivan, for example, while recognizing the psychodynamic roots of most psychoses, would still claim that there was a physical substrate in manic-depression. The periodicity of mood changes has seemed so baffling and opaque to many clinicians that there is an appeal to the body, as if this in itself were enough to answer the question of the timing and rhythm of manias and depressions.

Yet it is this very impasse that provides the clue. Questioned as to why an episode began when it did so often produces a non-response, as if no cause or trigger were apparent. Moods change with no apparent link to any external cause. But perhaps the connection here is exactly the failure to connect. Doctors in the 40s described what Freud's student Sándor Ferenczi had called 'anniversary reactions', whereby a physical symptom would appear on the anniversary of a significant date. The key was that the person would make no connection between the dates. The symptom appeared precisely because the memory didn't.

A woman woke up one morning with a searing pain in her back. She was unable to move, and for the next few months she was seen by doctors and consultants in an effort to diagnose what was wrong and find a remedy. She mentioned to one of the physiotherapists who visited her that she had been having nightmares, and he suggested to her that she contact me for a chat. This was a conversation and certainly not an analysis, and one of the first things I asked was whether the date on which she had woken up with the paralysis was significant to her. She thought about it for a while and then replied negatively.

As for the nightmares, these were variations on a single theme: she would be trying to close a suitcase or gather her bags, but always failing. When she spoke about her history, the dreams took on a particular resonance. As a child during the war, she had been forced to make a decision that effectively meant leaving her mother, who she would not see for decades. Weren't the nightmares in fact scenarios of not being able to leave? The failure to close the suitcases or gather the bags meant that she could not go anywhere.

When we now returned to the question of dates she was both horrified and amazed to realize that the date on which she had woken up with the paralysis was the very date on which she had left her mother in the war. The guilt at leaving had generated the symptom, but what was so striking here was the initial failure to see any significance in the date when I had asked her directly. It was only after the subsequent dialogue that the connection became clear. The symptom had emerged at the exact point where she had failed to connect two things.

In its very simplest form, isn't a mood just that: the failure to connect two ideas? If we wake up with a dark, nervous mood we might later realize it is because of a phone call we'll have to make that day or perhaps a dream we'd had during the night. The mood won't dissipate until the connection is made. The writer Rebecca West would always fall into a painful, wistful sadness when she saw mountain ranges, and it was only when she connected this to the graphs of the rise and fall of copper share prices that her father would anxiously scrutinize at breakfast when she was a child that her mood would evaporate.

The ahistorical nature of many accounts of manic-depression supports this idea. Jamison's childhood is described as happy and uneventful in the very same pages where we read of dramatic incidents and a parent who could be construed as manifestly unwell. Although the two threads are there, the connection between them is absent. Yet the more that history is foreclosed, the more that the swings of manic-depression will seem arbitrary and contingent, as if biology alone were the name of the body's clock. We could, on the contrary, see these swings as the result of a difficulty in inscribing history, often gravitating around a point of impossibility where something cannot be symbolized or processed psychically.

We could think here of the loss of Stephen Fry's ancestors in the Holocaust or the strange references to the camps in Andy Behrman's memoir. The latter in fact opens with a kind of shopping list of twenty-five items, ranging from 'Tanning salon', 'Pick up lithium and Prozac' to 'Buy a dog', yet including the seemingly incongruous 'Visit Auschwitz' and 'Make Holocaust documentary'. Fromm-Reichmann and her colleagues had emphasized the way in which the manic-depressive may be counted on to raise the prestige of the family or clan in a hostile world, both guided and crushed by the ideals of success and integration. And isn't this so often accompanied by the imperative to forget one's history, to rise above the past? Then, in manic-depression, it returns with a vengeance.

We see this quite literally in Patty Duke's case. Separated from her family at an early age by a couple eager to manage her acting career, she was told one day that her name would have to vanish: 'Anna Maria is dead,' they told her: 'You're Patty now.' Even her speech and accent would have to be refashioned, as she was turned into a Stepford child, instructed precisely on what to say and do and being forced to practise for several hours each day. 'I was stripped of my parents, I was stripped of my name, I was eventually stripped of my religion, and they had a blank slate to do with as they wished.' Is it surprising to see how her history would then return in the form of her acute highs and lows in later years?

This question of history is also clear in Jane Pauley's case. Her first mania was supposedly the result of a prescription for an antidepressant and a steroid for a bizarre attack of hives. If this explanation seemed self-evident, given the fact that both of these drugs are associated with triggering manic episodes, Pauley could not have been entirely satisfied. 'It occurred to me to find out what I had been working on at *Dateline* at the time the hives first reappeared. Scrolling back to my March 1999 computer files, I found a dozen files with the same name: "Daddy".'

The context of this was her participation in a TV programme called *Roots*, examining her family history. She remembered that she had been thinking of her father during her first night in hospital, and her hives had appeared most aggressively as she was reading Moss Hart's memoir, *Act One*. Her curiosity had been aroused by this book as it had lain on her father's bedside table for several years, and when she eventually went back to it after the emergence of her symptoms, the line immediately after the point she had stopped reading was 'I broke out in hives.' Pauley realized that her symptoms were linked to a mourning for her dead father.

Pauley's reconstruction of her history allows an understanding of the emergence of her manic episodes, and the autobiographical work of writers like Cheney and Fry shows how the apparently arbitrary cycles of manic-depression are never accidental. There is a difficulty here of integrating history, as if the links to one's past cannot be meaningfully subsumed. And hence the apparently ahistorical nature of manic-depression: the mood swings just seem sometimes to come out of nowhere.

If at times these can be clearly correlated to anniversary dates – a black depression coming in the month that one had lost a loved one many years previously – they also trigger at moments when an unintegratable element appears in that person's life, such as the rage towards a loved one that cannot be easily processed or a reminder of a guilt that has never been properly inscribed. The denominator here is a floating sense of responsibility, frequently for a death, that is summoned at such moments yet can never be entirely grasped or pinned down. The problem in integrating these elements generates a pervasive sense of, precisely, integration, when, in mania, everything makes sense, everything seems connected. But this tends to slide back towards a hole as the arc of mania moves on.

Might this suggest that the prevalence of so-called 'bipolarity' today is not simply an artefact of the marketing of the new diagnostic categories by pharmaceutical companies? We live in an age which pays lip service to history, yet which continually undermines the ties we have to the past. The narrative of human lives is more or less absent in healthcare economies, where symptoms are seen as problems to be treated locally, rather than as signs that something is wrong at a more fundamental level. Is it an accident that ECT, seen as the horizon of all other treatments for manic-depression, is essentially something that operates on human memory, a way to wipe out history?

We could evoke here a tragic encounter seen in a TV documentary about manic-depression. A woman whose mania triggered after the birth of her first child and who wants another baby consults an 'expert' and apparently learns what her risks are. She is worried about another serious manic episode, and, although as viewers we are not party to their discussion, the psychiatrist tells the programme's presenter about the dangers of childbirth as a triggering event and the statistics on postpartum suicide. We see her leave the building and hear her voice her decision not to have another child, given the risks that this would involve.

What we don't hear about are the reasons for her previous triggering, and we might wonder whether, if these had been explored properly, a strategy could have been formulated to allow her to avoid another manic episode at that moment. Instead, it seems as if her life has been reduced to a statistical paradigm with all sense of human history and meaning removed from it. External numerical data can tell her what her risks are without the weeks and months of dialogue that might produce a truer picture and allow her also to change the destiny that statistics dictate.

Such prejudices are echoed in an equally disturbing scene when Jamison visited a medical school to talk about manic-depression. Asked what their choices would be if a genetic test were available that predicted manic-depression in their child, nearly all the students, interns and staff in the room said that they would abort their foetus. As Emily Martin points out, this suggests that there is effectively an incompatibility between manic-depression and human life.

We should not forget here that traditionally manic-depression was seen as the one form of psychosis that was most likely to stabilize and resolve over time, whereas today it has almost the opposite reputation. This is surely linked to the abdication from efforts to understand the world of the manic-depressive in favour of an approach that aims to manage and control an apparently biological illness. It has been argued, indeed, that recovery rates were better in the pre-drug era, whereas today a diagnosis of manic-depression is almost certain to lead to a heavy regime of medication and, in many cases, prognostic bleakness. This is in marked, massive contrast to the psychiatry of the past.

Rather than becoming increasingly and exclusively obsessed with the fine-tuning of medication, we need to situate the life of the manic-depressive subject in context, exploring the detail of the highs and the lows and resisting the easy option of a blanket appeal to biology. Manic-depression must be carefully distinguished from vague and unhelpful notions of bipolar spectrum disorders, and diagnosed through its signature motifs: the flight of ideas, the special sense of connectedness to the world, the oscillation of a fault, and the effort to create a categorical separation of good and bad. The fact that the very time required to do this is generally denied even to those clinicians who wish to pursue such an approach is troubling. The airbrushing away of history and particularity echo the conditions of manic-depression itself.

The weight here of the marketing of bipolar should not be underestimated. As references to it multiply and as studies presuppose its existence as a valid diagnostic category, it becomes equated with an immutable biological entity. More and more people come to see themselves as bipolar, suffering from a 'disorder' that follows its own set of externally classified rules. One of the results of this is that the specificity of each case is lost, as we saw above with the example of the woman who felt discouraged from having another child, as if all cases were the same. The meaning that each individual might give to the events of their life vanishes as they become just another instantiation of an 'illness'.

With time being today's essential commodity, and with meaning seen as an irritating distraction to 'scientific' healthcare, people are deprived of the opportunity to explore their past in the context of their current difficulties. If the constellation of the manic-depressive includes within it a basic fault line here – an impossibility or even a refusal to inscribe oneself in some aspect of one's history – society's neglect of this dimension can only exacerbate their problems. We need to return to an earlier, more humane, approach; one which attends to the particularity of each case, and which offers the manic-depressive person the chance to assume – however slowly, however painfully – what can be assumed of their history, and to find a way to live with what can't.

Notes

pp. 1–2 Statistics, see C. Moreno et al., 'National trends in the outpatient diagnosis and treatment of bipolar disorder in youth', *Archives of General Psychiatry*, 64 (2007), pp. 1032–9; Kathryn Burrows, 'What epidemic? The social construction of bipolar epidemics', *Advances in Medical Sociology*, 11 (2010), pp. 243–61; and David Healy, *Mania: A Short History of Bipolar Disorder* (Baltimore: Johns Hopkins, 2008). The question today, see Kathryn Burrows, 'What epidemic?', op. cit., p. 250. On bipolar, the media and the markets, see Emily Martin, *Bipolar Expeditions: Mania and Depression in American Culture* (New Jersey: Princeton University Press, 2007). Turner, see Emily Martin, *Bipolar Expeditions*, op. cit., p. 208.

pp. 3–6 History, see Antoine Ritti, 'Traité clinique de la folie à double forme: Folie circulaire, délire à formes alternes' (Paris: Octave Doin, 1883); L. Linas, 'Manie', *Dictionnaire encylopédique des sciences médicales* (Paris: Asselin, 1871), pp. 507–60; P. L. Couchoud, 'Histoire de la manie jusqu'à Kraepelin', *Revue des sciences psychologiques*, 1 (1913), pp. 149–73; German Berrios, 'Mood Disorders', in German Berrios and Roy Porter (eds), *A History of Clinical Psychiatry* (London: Athlone Press, 1995), pp. 384–408; Lisa Hermsen, *Manic Minds: Mania's Mad History and Its Neuro-Future* (New Brunswick: Rutgers University Press, 2011); and David Healy, *Mania*, op. cit. On marketing of diagnostic categories, see

David Healy, *The Antidepressant Era* (Cambridge, Mass.: Harvard University Press, 1997). A case study of marketing bipolar can be found in Andrew Lakoff, *Pharmaceutical Reason: Knowledge and Value in Global Psychiatry* (Cambridge: Cambridge University Press, 2005). Drugs, see Joanna Moncrieff, *The Myth of the Chemical Cure* (London: Macmillan, 2009); and Des Spence, 'Bad Medicine: Bipolar 2 Disorder', *British Medical Journal*, 342 (2011), p. 2767. New brand, see Christopher Lane, 'Bipolar disorder and its biomythology: An interview with David Healy', *Psychology Today* (16 April 2009).

pp. 6–7 Jules Baillarger, 'Note sur un genre de folie dont les accès sont caractérisés par deux périodes régulières, l'une de dépression, l'autre d'excitation', *Bulletin de l'Académie Nationale de Médicine*, 19 (1853–4), pp. 340–52; 'Réponse à Falret', ibid., pp. 401–15; and Jean-Pierre Falret, 'Mémoire sur la folie circulaire', ibid., pp. 382–400. On the Falret–Baillarger debate, see P. Pichot, 'The birth of bipolar disorder', *European Psychiatry*, 10 (1995), pp. 1–10. On the question of differential diagnosis, see Eugen Bleuler, 'Die Probleme der Schizoidie und der Syntonie', *Zeitschrift für die gesamte Neurologie und Psychiatrie*, 78 (1922), pp. 373–99; G. Halberstadt, 'Syndromes anormaux au cours de la psychose maniaco-dépressive', *Annales Médico-Psychologiques*, 88 (1930), pp. 117–42; and Darian Leader, 'On the Specificity of Manic-Depressive Psychosis', in Patricia Gherovici and Manya Steinkoler (eds), *The Method in Madness: Lacanian Approaches to Insanity* (forthcoming: London: Routledge, 2014).

pp. 7–9 Jean-Étienne Esquirol, *Des maladies mentales considérées sous les rapports médical, hygiénique et médico-légal* (Paris: Baillière, 1838); Emil Kraepelin, *Psychiatrie: Ein Lehrbuch für*

Studierende und Aerzte, 6th edn, (Leipzig: Barth, 1899). Partial translation of 8th edn in Kraepelin, *Manic-Depressive Insanity and Paranoia* (Edinburgh: Livingstone, 1921). See the collection of critiques in A. Rémond and P. Voivenel, 'Essai sur la valeur de la conception kraepelinienne de la manie et de la mélancolie', *Annales Médico-Psychologiques*, 12 (1910), pp. 353–79; and ibid. (1911), pp. 19–51.

pp. 9–10 Andy Behrman, *Electroboy: A Memoir of Mania* (New York: Random House, 2002), p. 261; Lizzie Simon, *Detour: My Bipolar Road Trip in 4-D* (New York: Simon & Schuster, 2002), p. 187.

p. 11 Parcel, see David Healy, *Mania*, op. cit., p. 239.

pp. 12–13 Andy Behrman, *Electroboy*, op. cit., pp. xiv and xxi; Terri Cheney, *Manic: A Memoir* (New York: Harper, 2008), p. 212; and Stephen Fry, Foreword to Jeremy Thomas and Tony Hughes, *You Don't Have to be Famous to Have Manic Depression* (London: Michael Joseph, 2006), p. 7. Terri Cheney, *Manic*, op. cit., p. 146.

p. 15 Lizzie Simon, *Detour*, op. cit., p. 121. Brian Adams, *The Pits and the Pendulum: A Life with Bipolar Disorder* (London: Jessica Kingsley, 2003), p. 79.

p. 16 Calvin Dunn, *Losing My Mind: Chronicle of Bipolar Mania* (Philadelphia: Infinity, 2012), p. 81. Kay Redfield Jamison, *An Unquiet Mind: A Memoir of Moods and Madness* (New York: Knopf, 1995), pp. 42–3.

p. 18 Tie, see Ernest Jones, 'Psychoanalytic notes on a case of hypomania', *American Journal of Insanity*, 2 (1911), pp. 203–18.

pp. 19–20 Language and flight of ideas, see Ludwig Binswanger, 'Sur la fuite des idées' (1932) (Paris: Millon, 2000); Hugo Liepmann, *Über Ideenflucht* (Halle: Marhold, 1904); Max Isserlin, 'Psychologische Untersuchungen an

Manisch-Depressiven', *Monatsschrift für Psychiatrie und Neurologie*, 22 (1907), pp. 338–55, 419–42 and 509–22; Maria Lorenz and Stanley Cobb, 'Language behaviour in manic patients', *Archives of Neurology and Psychiatry*, 69 (1953), pp. 763–70; and Stanley Newman and Vera Mather, 'Analysis of spoken language of patients with affective disorders', *American Journal of Psychiatry*, 94 (1938), pp. 913–42. Norma Farnes, *Spike: An Intimate Memoir* (London: HarperCollins, 2004), p. 4.

p. 21 Patty Duke and Gloria Hochman, *A Brilliant Madness: Living with Manic-Depressive Illness* (New York: Bantam, 1992), p. 12; Lisa Hermsen, *Manic Minds*, op. cit., p. 94; and Terri Cheney, *The Dark Side of Innocence: Growing Up Bipolar* (New York: Atria, 2011), p. 170.

pp. 22–4 Andy Behrman, *Electroboy*, op. cit., p. 258. Leigh, see Alexander Walker, *Vivien: The Life of Vivien Leigh* (London: Weidenfeld, 1987), p. 372; and Hugo Vickers, *Vivien Leigh* (London: Hamish Hamilton, 1988). Patty Duke and Gloria Hochman, *A Brilliant Madness*, op. cit., p. 163. Terri Cheney, *Manic*, op. cit., pp. 7 and 68.

pp. 25–6 Freud, *Jokes and Their Relation to the Unconscious* (1905), *Standard Edition*, vol. 8, pp. 9–238; *Humour* (1927), *Standard Edition*, vol. 21, pp. 161–6; and Isador Coriat, 'Humor and hypomania', *Psychiatric Quarterly*, 13 (1939), pp. 681–8. On the third party in jokes, see Jacques Lacan, *Les Formations de l'Inconscient* (1957–8), ed. J.-A. Miller (Paris: Seuil, 1998).

pp. 27–8 Terri Cheney, *The Dark Side of Innocence*, op. cit. Kay Redfield Jamison, *An Unquiet Mind*, op. cit., pp. 11, 16 and 90–91.

p. 29 Andy Behrman, *Electroboy*, op. cit., p. 169. Emil Kraepelin, *Manic-Depressive Insanity and Paranoia*, op. cit., p. 57.

pp. 30–31 Wilhelm Griesinger, *Mental Pathology and Therapeutics*, 2nd edn (1861) (New York: Hafner, 1965), pp. 273–318.

Henri Ey, 'Manie', *Études psychiatriques*, vol. 3 (Paris: Desclée de Brouwer, 1954), pp. 47–116; and 'Les Psychoses périodiques maniaco-dépressives', ibid., pp. 430–518. Stephen Fry, *The Fry Chronicles: An Autobiography* (London: Michael Joseph, 2010), p. 109. Lizzie Simon, *Detour*, op. cit., p. 108.

pp. 31–3 Emily Martin, *Bipolar Expeditions*, op. cit., p. 217. Katharine Graham, *Personal History* (New York: Random House, 1997). Jane Pauley, *Skywriting: A Life Out of the Blue* (New York: Random House, 2004), p. 9. TV producer, see Jeremy Thomas and Tony Hughes, *You Don't Have to be Famous to Have Manic Depression*, op. cit., p. 142.

p. 34 Brian Adams, *The Pits and the Pendulum*, op. cit., pp. 61–2 and 76–7. Emily Martin, *Bipolar Expeditions*, op. cit., p. 206.

pp. 35–6 Mabel Blake Cohen et al., 'An intensive study of 12 cases of manic-depressive psychosis', *Psychiatry*, 17 (1954), pp. 103–37; and Frieda Fromm-Reichmann, 'Intensive psychotherapy of manic-depressives', *Confinia Neurologica*, 9 (1949), pp. 158–65. Car taking off, James Hamilton, 'The critical effect of object loss in the development of episodic manic illness', *Journal of the American Academy of Psychoanalysis and Dynamic Psychiatry*, 34 (2006), pp. 333–48.

pp. 36–7 Andy Behrman, *Electroboy*, op. cit., pp. 6 and 261.

pp. 38–9 Mulheren, see Connie Bruck, 'The World of Business: No One Like Me', *New Yorker* (11 March 1991), pp. 40–68. Lizzie Simon, *Detour*, op. cit., p. 69. Kay Redfield Jamison, *An Unquiet Mind*, op. cit., pp. 76 and 83.

pp. 40–41 Stephen Fry, *The Fry Chronicles*, op. cit., p. 27; and *The Liar* (London: William Heinemann, 1991), p. 167.

pp. 43–4 Kay Redfield Jamison, *An Unquiet Mind*, op. cit., pp. 12–13. Belief in good Other, see Edith Jacobson, 'Contribution to the metapsychology of cyclothymic depressions', in Phyllis

Greenacre (ed.), *Affective Disorders* (New York: International Universities Press, 1953), pp. 49–83.

pp. 44–5 See Melanie Klein, 'A Contribution to the Psychogenesis of Manic-Depressive States' (1935), in *Contributions to Psycho-Analysis* (London: Hogarth, 1948), pp. 282–310; and 'Mourning and Its Relation to Manic-Depressive States' (1940), ibid., pp. 311–38. Edith Jacobson, 'Contribution', op. cit., p. 74. Terri Cheney, *The Dark Side of Innocence*, op. cit., p. 182. Eugen Bleuler, *Textbook of Psychiatry* (1916) (New York: Macmillan, 1924), p. 468.

pp. 45–7 Oak, see Norma Farnes, *Spike*, op. cit., pp. 76–7. Patty Duke and Gloria Hochman, *A Brilliant Madness*, op. cit., p. 103.

pp. 47–8 Freud, *Notes upon a Case of Obsessional Neurosis* (1909), *Standard Edition*, vol. 10, p. 190. Theodor Reik, *Listening with the Third Ear* (New York: Grove Press, 1948). See the early comments on obsessional phenomena in manic-depression by K. Bonhoeffer, 'Über die Beziehungen der Zwangsvorstellungen zum Manisch-Depressiven Irresein', *Monatsschrift für Psychiatrie und Neurologie*, 33 (1913), pp. 354–8.

pp. 48–51 Stephen Fry, *The Fry Chronicles*, op. cit., pp. 7–20 and 28; and *Moab is My Washpot* (London: Hutchinson, 1997), p. 127.

pp. 51–2 Pausanias, *Descriptions of Greece*, 8.34.1. See also Cicero, *Tusculan Disputations*, 3.5.11. Abraham Brill, 'Unconscious insight: Some of its manifestations', *International Journal of Psychoanalysis*, 10 (1929), pp. 145–61.

pp. 52–6 Death, see John Thompson MacCurdy, *The Psychology of Emotion: Morbid and Normal* (London: Kegan Paul, 1925); and German Arce Ross, *Manie, mélancolie et facteurs blancs* (Paris: Beauchesne, 2009). Terri Cheney, *Manic*, op. cit., p. 169; Patty Duke and Gloria Hochman, *A Brilliant*

Madness, op. cit., p. 17; Leigh, see Alexander Walker, *Vivien*, op. cit. p. 181.

p. 57 Edward Glover, 'Medico-Psychological Aspects of Normality' (1932), in *On the Early Development of Mind: Collected Papers of Edward Glover* (London: Imago, 1956), p. 239.

pp. 58–60 Andy Behrman, *Electroboy*, op. cit., p. xix. Kay Redfield Jamison, *An Unquiet Mind*, op. cit., p. 74; Edith Jacobson, 'Contribution', op. cit., p. 74; Patty Duke and Gloria Hochman, *A Brilliant Madness*, op. cit., p. 113.

pp. 61–2 Wilhelm Griesinger, *Mental Pathology and Therapeutics*, op. cit., p. 281.

p. 62 Loss was indeed linked more frequently to mania in ancient literature than to depression: see Peter Toohey, 'Love, Lovesickness, and Melancholia', *Illinois Classical Studies*, 17 (1992), pp. 265–86.

pp. 62–4 Patty Duke and Gloria Hochman, *A Brilliant Madness*, op. cit., p. 17; and Melanie Klein, 'Mourning and Its Relation to Manic-Depressive States', op. cit. World as breast, see Bertram Lewin, *The Psychoanalysis of Elation* (London: Hogarth, 1951); and Panel, Midwinter Meetings (1950), *Bulletin of the American Psychoanalytic Association*, 7 (1951), pp. 229–76.

p. 64 Terri Cheney, *Manic*, op. cit., pp. 20 and 160.

p. 67 Frieda Fromm-Reichmann, 'Intensive psychotherapy', op. cit., p. 161; and Kay Redfield Jamison, *An Unquiet Mind*, op. cit., p. 118. See also Kay Redfield Jamison and Frederick Goodwin, *Manic-Depressive Illness: Bipolar Disorders and Recurrent Depression* (Oxford: Oxford University Press, 1990).

pp. 68–70 Patty Duke and Gloria Hochman, *A Brilliant Madness*, op. cit., p. 204. Paranoid trends, see Sándor Radó, 'Psychodynamics of depression', *Psychosomatic Medicine*, 13 (1951), pp. 51–5.

pp. 70–72 Cleaning, see Alexander Walker, *Vivien*, op. cit., pp. 266 and 307; Andy Behrman, *Electroboy*, op. cit., pp. 217–18; and Brian Adams, *The Pits and the Pendulum*, op. cit., p. 127.

p. 72 Psychoanalysis, see the discussion in Freud, *Mourning and Melancholia* (1917), *Standard Edition*, vol. 14, pp. 237–58. On the early analytic approaches, see Jules Masserman, 'Psychodynamisms in manic-depressive psychoses', *Psychoanalytic Review*, 28 (1941), pp. 466–78; and Joseph Blalock, 'Psychology of the manic phase of manic-depressive psychoses', *Psychiatric Quarterly*, 10 (1936), pp. 262–344. Andy Behrman, *Electroboy*, op. cit., p. xx.

pp. 72–3 Kay Redfield Jamison, *An Unquiet Mind*, op. cit., pp. 38 and 45.

p. 73 Spike Milligan, 'Manic Depression', quoted in Norma Farnes, *Spike*, op. cit., p. 80.

pp. 74–5 Patty Duke and Gloria Hochman, *A Brilliant Madness*, op. cit., p. 198. See Alexander Walker, *Vivien*, op. cit., p. 31.

pp. 76–8 Jane Pauley, *Skywriting*, op. cit., p. 4; Kay Redfield Jamison, *An Unquiet Mind*, op. cit., p. 182; Emil Kraepelin, *Manic-Depressive Insanity and Paranoia*, op. cit., p. 54; and Terri Cheney, *Manic*, op. cit., p. 184. Ibid., p. 188; and *The Dark Side of Innocence*, op. cit., p. 69.

p. 79 Darian Leader, 'The Depressive Position for Klein and Lacan', in *Freud's Footnotes* (London: Faber, 2000), pp. 189–236.

pp. 79–80 Sullivan, see Mabel Blake Cohen et al., 'An intensive study', op. cit.; and Patrick Mullahy, *Psychoanalysis and Interpersonal Psychiatry* (New York: Science House, 1970), p. 638.

pp. 80–81 Non-meaning of precipitating factors, see George Winokur et al., *Manic Depressive Illness* (Saint Louis: Mosby, 1969). Anniversary symptoms, see Darian Leader and David Corfield, *Why Do People Get Ill?* (London: Hamish Hamilton, 2007), pp. 83–93. Paul Schilder, 'Vorstudien zu einer Psychologie der Manie', *Zeitschrift für die gesamte Neurologie und Psychiatrie*, 68 (1921), pp. 90–135.

pp. 82–4 Patty Duke and Kenneth Turan, *Call Me Anna* (New York: Bantam, 1987), pp. 23 and 30. Jane Pauley, *Skywriting*, op. cit., pp. 24 and 237–8.

p. 86 Emily Martin, *Bipolar Expeditions*, op. cit., p. 12.

Acknowledgements

Thanks first of all to my patients, who have guided, corrected and encouraged me throughout the writing of this book. Several autobiographical accounts and studies of manic-depression have also been inspiring, and I have learned a lot from the works of Brian Adams, Andy Behrman, Terri Cheney, Stephen Fry, David Healy, Kay Redfield Jamison, Emily Martin and Lizzie Simon. I am very grateful to the friends and colleagues who have contributed to this book: Josh Appignanesi, Chloe Aridjis, Devorah Baum, Julia Carne, Louise Clarke, Sarah Clement, Vincent Dachy, Simon Finch, Astrid Gessert, Anouchka Grose, Hanif Kureishi, Renata Salecl, Will Sergeant, Christos Tombras and Jay Watts. Pat Blackett and Sophie Pathan gave me invaluable help with research, and Anna Kelly, Anna Ridley and Sarah Coward with the publication process. Simon Prosser was as ever a generous and sensitive editor; Tracy Bohan at Wylie a fabulous agent; and Mary Horlock a special and supportive reader.

DARIAN LEADER

THE NEW BLACK

How hard or easy is it to tell what happens when we lose someone we love? A death, a separation or the break-up of a relationship are some of the hardest times we have to live through. We may fall into a nightmare of depression, lose the will to live and see no hope for the future. What matters at this crucial point is whether or not we are able to mourn.

In this important and groundbreaking book, acclaimed psychoanalyst and writer Darian Leader urges us to look beyond the catch-all concept of depression to explore the deeper, unconscious ways in which we respond to the experience of loss. In so doing, we can loosen the grip it may have upon our lives.

'His orthodox, psychoanalytical approach produces an unpredictable, occasionally brilliant book. *The New Black* is a mixture of Freudian text, clinical assessments and Leader's own brand of gentle wisdom' *Herald*

'Compelling and important . . . an engrossing and wise book' **Hanif Kureishi**

'There are many self-help books on the market . . . *The New Black* is a book that might actually help' *Independent*

DARIAN LEADER

WHAT IS MADNESS?

What separates the sane from the mad? How hard or easy is it to tell them apart? And what if the difference is really between being mad and going mad?

In this landmark work Darian Leader undermines common conceptions of madness. Through case studies like that of the apparently 'normal' Harold Shipman, he shows that madness rarely conforms to the images we might expect. By exploring the idea of 'quiet madness' – that psychosis and an uneventful normal life are absolutely compatible – he argues that we must radically revise our understanding of madness.

'Provides valuable insights into how psychiatry can help those who have suffered psychosis to rebuild their lives' *Sunday Times*

'Witty, probing. A myth-busting diagnosis of the method in our madness' *Independent*

'Leader's insights could have radical consequences for the way we regard madness' *Daily Telegraph*